Mentoring
in Early Childhood
Settings

by Arlene Martin
& Polly Ashelman

Mentoring

in Early Childhood Settings

Arlene Martin
& Polly Ashelman

KENDALL/HUNT PUBLISHING COMPANY
4050 Westmark Drive   Dubuque, Iowa 52002

The authors dedicate this book to the many professionals who have provided us with the mentoring models necessary to frame our path. We are indebted to all our teachers who have inspired us with their wisdom.

Contents

Foreword

The key to quality in early childhood settings is the quality of relationships – relationships between the child and the family, between child and caregiver, between caregiver and family and among adults in the child care setting. Child care quality depends on caregivers who are knowledgeable and skilled, and committed to creating and sustaining these relationships (Lally, Griffin, Fenichel, Segal, Szanton & Weissbourd, 1995).

How do early childhood professionals learn to establish and maintain mutually satisfying, growth-promoting relationships with very young children, families, and colleagues? All too often, early childhood professionals are left to learn these crucial skills on their own in a career-long process of trial and error. The beginning child care provider wonders how to reach out effectively to a parent from another culture or a parent under obvious stress. The seasoned child care professional, perhaps newly promoted to a director's position, may have an equally difficult time trying to support the professional development of her staff or evaluate their performance.

As Arlene Martin and Polly Ashelman demonstrate so clearly in this important and eminently useful book, such solitary struggles need not be the inevitable feature of work in the field of early care and education. We can learn how protégés strengthen relationships *through* relationships. Mentoring relationships, in particular, offer both mentors and their protégés regular opportunities to learn from each other in mutually rewarding, reciprocal ways – exactly as one would hope that infants and parents, caregivers and children, parents and professionals, and colleagues with different levels of experience learn from each other in relationships.

Demonstrating their lively understanding of adult learning styles, Martin and Ashelman offer the reader many ways to explore mentoring as a relationship for learning. They review the research on mentoring; present models in mentoring in preservice training as well as in on-the job professional development; and describe nuts-and-bolts strategies and lessons learned from efforts to establish mentoring programs in a multi-site center-based child care organizations and a network of family care providers. Interviews with five mentor/protégé dyads – a vivid example of what one student of mentoring calls "affectionate research" – illustrate qualities of attentiveness, nonjudgement, integrity, trustfulness, and kindness that contribute to make mentoring relationships vehicles for transformational learning. Throughout the book, the authors suggest activities to assist the reader who is considering, planning, implementing, or participating in a mentoring relationship or program.

As the field of early care and education continues on its quest for quality – rightly emphasizing the importance of practitioners' professional development – this volume will serve as a trustworthy guide.

Emily Fenichel & Linda Eggbeer
Zero to Three/The National Center
for Clinical Infant Programs

Acknowledgements

We thank those who have made this book possible, funders of the Kean University/Montclair State University Collaborative for Child Care Training in New Jersey, the Prudential Foundation, the Schumann Fund, and the Victoria Foundation. Special thanks to Eileen Howell-Lee of the Collaborative for Child Care Training in New Jersey, for her training and mentoring expertise as co-director of this project.

We thank those who are responsible for our preparation as trainers, leaders and advocates in the field of early care and education. A special thanks to our colleagues at Zero to Three, the National Center for Clinical Infant Programs, Washington, D.C. whose influence shaped the training approaches shared in this book.

To our colleagues, Elyse Barbell Rudolph, for preparation of staff development exercises and David Spivak of Design Solutions for his creative development. Our sincere appreciation to Joyce Richardson and Lynn Wu for their excellent preparation of our manuscript and to June Moss Handler, Maxine Fischel and Elizabeth Carlson for review of our manuscript.

Finally, our thanks to the mentor and protégé voices heard in these chapters. We appreciate all your stories.

Introduction

I n its first edition, *Building Literacy Through Child Development* (Restaino-Kelly & Barbell Rudolph, 1997), the paraprofessional in early childhood takes a journey through several aspects of professional development. In this companion book, *Mentoring in Early Childhood Settings* (1999), designed for program directors, education specialists, or mentor teachers, the journey continues to support the role of professional development. The goal of this text is to assist in the process of staff development, through the use of mentoring in early childhood settings. This book serves to document the DART Mentor Teacher Model, which was developed through the DART Center at Kean University.

The DART Center, which stands for Dissemination, Advocacy, Research and Training, was established in 1990 through the efforts of child care professionals in New Jersey, who served on the Coalition of Infant/Toddler Educators (CITE), a statewide advocacy organization. Initially, the Coalition approached the Department of Early Childhood and Family Studies at Kean University in New Jersey to gain support for the development of a center for infant/family studies which would sponsor research and training efforts. Funding was secured for a three-year pilot project through the Prudential Foundation, The Schumann Fund for New Jersey, the A.T.&T Family Development Fund, Mutual of New York, and the Victoria Foundation.

During this three-year project, thirty-six supervisors took part in a comprehensive nine-month program, with 12 participants in each of the 3 years. The training included 60 hours of seminars and 25 hours of supervised field experiences. The supervisors were each paired with a field trainer, who was a master-teacher. The master-teacher/supervisory relationship included mentoring, coaching and supervising, which was later identified as the most critical component of the training.

The DART Mentor Teaching Model and subsequent adaptations of the model are described throughout this book. Chapter One describes the DART Model and its distinguishing features, focusing on professional development. Chapter two presents an overview of the literature on mentoring and emphasizes adult development. Chapter Three provides profiles of two agencies which adapted the DART Mentor Teacher Model to their specific center staff needs for on-site team building. Chapter Four explores the role of mentor/teacher consultants as key figures in the assistance and support of program accreditation. The role of the mentor/teacher as a professional staff developer is a prominent feature of the DART Mentor Teacher Model. It leads the authors to more recent in-depth research on mentoring relationships.

In Chapter Five, an alumni mentoring project in an early childhood graduate program is described. It also addresses how portfolios, book arts and documentation are used to build professionalism. Chapter Six presents profiles of five mentor/protégé dyads taken from research conducted to demonstrate the depth and effect of mentoring on the participant's personal and professional growth. In Chapter Seven, we provide insights on effective staff development and its relationship to the improvement of program quality. This chapter emphasizes mentoring approaches based on the concept of transformational learning, and offers implications on using mentoring models in the field of early care and education.

Throughout this book, the concepts and applications of mentoring are introduced to the reader. The authors hope that as program directors and staff developers, supervisors and administrators, the reader will be to able incorporate these ideas and strategies to professionalize staff and to improve program quality.

The authors encourage the reader to reflect on, integrate and adapt these ideas to suit individual and staff needs. Mentoring "lessons" can be integrated into most staff development programs through a variety of training techniques. Some of the mentoring "lessons learned" are examined within this text. The reader is invited to contextualize these ideas within his/her own early childhood settings.

Mentoring in Staff Development

In *Building Literacy Through Child Development* (1997), students were encouraged to seek a mentor they respected to assist them in their professional development journey. This book examines mentoring as a support system for staff. Staff often need a more senior person to answer questions, give advice, provide information about policy, curriculum, and guidance, or observe them in their teaching role. Isolation of novice teachers is a problem common to staff in all types of educational settings. In early childhood, this is a pervasive problem. Adults, who work with young children, need the support, encouragement and acknowledgement of others in similar roles. They also need someone to model developmentally appropriate practices (DAP) and to address their psycho-social needs. A mentor serves as a model for good practice. For this reason, the best mentors are individuals who have achieved a high level of professional development.

A mentor may make the difference between a teacher leaving the early childhood field or making it a career for life. This book advocates the use of mentoring as a process for profound personal and professional change through transformational learning. Martin, 1998 views transformational learning as a shift in one's meaning connection or understanding. "It is something that makes a fundamental difference in how people change their practice" (Fischel, 1998). It also includes applications of mentoring models in early childhood programs, and serves to assist supervisors, directors and administrators in becoming mentors to staff. The following section introduces a discussion of staff development issues common to the field of children as they relate to mentoring.

Developing a Professional Self

For anyone who delivers child care training, there are a variety of reasons why staff development does not occur consistently. Usually these issues or concerns deter the process and may often seem justifiable. However, lack of ongoing staff development prevents a program from achieving uniform quality. In the child care field, staff are usually at differing levels of development which makes staff development an ongoing challenge. This text will assist in making this challenge into a positive experience as new staff learn to use the valuable resources of their more experienced colleagues through mentoring.

Adult Development

In Chapter Two, Understanding the Research on Mentoring, the literature on adult development is discussed. Adult development is a dynamic process, and adults learn best in interactive sessions, which offer a variety of teaching strategies to promote critical thinking and inquiry. These strategies may range from mini-lecture to individual and group exercises, and should focus on helping adults accept and internalize new information through active processes. Adults also learn best when their own experience base is drawn upon, and they relate well to examples of practices common to them. Jones (1993) includes teacher narrative or teacher story telling as a way of knowing and of transforming. She theorizes that when adults realize their "voice there is a moving from silence to a connected and constructed knowledge" (29). Using adult experiences helps to relate theory to practice and is a major goal of staff development. Therefore, an important strategy in professionalizing staff is to provide developmental information or child development theory as a part of training meetings. This technique can be adapted to any staff development session. It is an effective means for explaining theory in more familiar terms, and it also often results in greater bonding within the group. Furthermore, it gives staff developers an opportunity to dispel or correct misapplications of the child development information under discussion.

Goals for Professionalizing Staff

Integrated into each chapter are goals for professionalizing staff using mentoring approaches. The underlying goal of any staff development program is to provide staff access to ongoing in-service training, which includes conferences, workshops and web technology. All staff need to meet regularly to share information and concerns, to address curriculum issues, and to discuss children. Staff meetings are prime opportunities to build developmental knowledge, to raise issues concerning developmentally appropriate practices (DAP) and to brainstorm with staff around specific areas of concern such as guidance or health/safety. Staff meetings should be held at a consistent and convenient time each month, and they should have a specified agenda. The more organized, consistent and informed staff become as a result of staff meetings; the more they will want to continue on their professional development path.

Whenever possible staff members should be included in the delivery of training so that they can contribute their own special expertise. At each staff meeting, a staff member may be asked on a rotational basis to prepare an exercise or activity to share with their peers. In this way, all staff are involved over time and affirmed in their experience base. Staff members' self-esteem increases as they get a chance to showcase their unique curriculum ideas or novel approaches to working with young children. Staff will appreciate having opportunities to share information with their peers. The positive overtones of this practice will, in turn, ease staff members' movement into larger professional development events outside of their worksite. With the provision of appropriate support, staff will look forward to training meetings and professional development initiatives.

On-Site Team Building

Team building is an important component of high quality child care programs. Chapters Three, Mentoring Initiatives: Two Case Studies on Mentoring, and Four, Applying a Mentor/Teacher Consultant Model to the Accreditation

Process, relate examples of on-site team building using mentoring models in a variety of early childhood settings. Child care centers are structured as a family unit, so individuals cannot do their job in isolation, unless they are providing one-on-one care or in-home family child care. However, even in family child care settings, the provider needs support and resources from the outside community in order to provide high quality experiences for children. In a child care setting, a team approach is absolutely necessary. Part of a staff developer's role is to model team building strategies for staff, and to provide strategies that promote a cooperative working environment. It is often a challenge for staff developers to overcome the hierarchy of roles which are in place in most child care settings, such as program director, head teacher, teacher, lead teacher, group teacher, assistant teacher and teacher aide. While role designations are important to a program's organizational structure, staff developers must create partnerships so that learning is reciprocal. Roles and tasks should be interchangeable. Team building for staff meetings may also identify who needs help and how support can be provided, so that no one is feeling isolated.

The exercises included in this text provide some opportunities to develop team-building skills. They are designed to be used in staff meetings and should be helpful in creating bonds among staff. They will also assist in bridging the divisions between preschool and infant/toddler staff, which sometimes occur because of the differences in caregiving responsibilities between the two groups. Other forms of staff development techniques to promote professional growth are described throughout the text.

Assessment of Staff - Using Portfolios to Support Professional Development

Staff developers not only provide training, but may assess staff as well. It takes a skilled and balanced professional to conduct a purposeful and effective assessment process for staff. Many staff developers or administrators do not have enough time to conduct staff assessment adequately. There are numerous ways to assess staff, for example through checklists, anecdotal observations, or narrative descriptions. Staff assessment should not only provide a measure of performance, but also inform trainers of areas in which staff members need individual support in order to continue professional development. Self-assessment is also a valuable skill for developing professionals. Regular journal writing, portfolios and peer observations assist staff in evaluation of their own work.

Use of Portfolio

Portfolios provide an informal means for staff assessment. They are documents used to demonstrate professional growth of the individual staff member. In educational settings, they have become acceptable and valuable tools for authentic assessment of both children and staff. Teacher portfolios often contain a variety of documents to tell a story about a person's professional growth.

Staff developers in all early childhood settings are advised to create opportunities for staff to use portfolios to document their professional development. Child Development Associate (CDA) candidates, who must produce a written resource file in order to be formally assessed, are developing one form of a portfolio. With some minor adaptations, a CDA resource file can be utilized to create a portfolio for professional development.

Some examples of documentation in portfolios include an autobiography, journals and personal reflections, photos of the staff member/children and classroom, curriculum samples, artifacts or artwork, letters of recommendation from parents, administrators or other professionals; certificates of workshops attended, conferences or conference presentations; transcripts of coursework taken, and copies of professional degrees or credentials. Staff may be encouraged to be as creative or innovative as possible and to include a wide variety of documents to support professional growth.

The presentation of portfolios is also very important, and staff should be given an in-service session to learn creative ways to develop and showcase their portfolios. This process will lead to an active staff meeting. The act of developing a portfolio is not only engaging but also promotes growth of self-esteem and confidence. Staff begin to learn to appreciate their own gifts, as they collect and document their ongoing personal story of growth.

These strategies and techniques promote opportunities to professionalize staff and "grow teachers" (Jones, 1993). Mentors use these strategies with staff to build the mentor/protégé relationship. The following chapter introduces the DART Mentor Teacher Model. It discusses the model in greater detail, and it emphasizes the importance of relationship learning.

Building a Mentoring Model

The DART Mentor Teacher Model – from Theory to Practice

Chapter 1

T he child care field continues to struggle with the challenges of how to provide high quality care for young children, particularly those from birth to three years of age. Poorly prepared staff, inadequate standards of care, problems of high staff turnover, low wages and benefits, and sub-standard working conditions for the predominately female child care workforce are continuing issues. Because of the inadequate quality of child care staff, centers may actually compromise children's intellectual and emotional development (Hofferth, 1991, 1996; Frede, 1995; Kagan, 1997; Barnett and Boocock, 1998). However, there is hope for changing these conditions and making progress toward professionalizing the field through consistent and systematic training of child care staff.

Professional development in early care and education presents the field with new challenges and promising practices. Innovative initiatives, such as mentoring for staff development, are gaining recognition as important components of program accreditation (Martin, 1998). With the continuing commitment of teacher preparation programs to define and uphold standards and to provide supervision and mentoring, quality improvement in the field of early care and education will be attained. This chapter describes the DART Mentor Teacher Model, a staff development program, which includes mentoring as a central feature of its design.

The DART
Training Model

In the DART Center's original pilot project, the training model was called the DART Training of Trainers. Subsequently it became known as the DART Mentor Teacher Model. Its goal was to increase the quality of care for infants and toddlers through improving the competency of child care supervisors. In turn these supervisors became master-teachers and mentors to their caregiver staff. Training was intended to enhance the overall quality of life in a center or a family child care program, by improving caregiver-supervisor interactions and increasing the effectiveness of center supervision through staff development. Assessment of the effectiveness of the DART Mentor Teacher Model, (Ferrar 1994) indicated supervisors of infant/toddler child care programs who participated as protégés paired with field mentors had a powerful effect on relationship learning. Supervisors (protégés) showed improvement in their supervisory skills, teacher practice, and quality of adult/child interactions. They also increased their self-confidence and self-esteem as they became better practitioners.

The DART Mentor Teacher Model is comprised of 3 strands; adult development, interactional dynamics, and mentoring/supervisory processes. These curriculum areas provide the training base for the model and serve as linkages for transmitting training across all levels of staff. Through this training, supervisors gain understandings in the areas of:

- adult personality development and learning styles.
- child development and appropriate child care practices.
- supervisory processes.
- interactional dynamics, as they define quality relationships.

When it was piloted in urban child care centers between 1991-1994, the DART Mentor Teacher Model was presented in fourteen seminars over a nine month period, and it included a supervised training experience of 85 hours. This interval allowed time for ideas to be absorbed and new techniques to be practiced. In addition, it provided enough space for mentor/protégé relationships to grow.

The seminar series began with study of the concept of adult personality development and included interpreting the results of the Meyers-Briggs Personality Inventory, which was administered to all participants. Stages of adult and teacher development and adult learning styles followed. Assessment of the child care center environment was emphasized. For this purpose, supervisors were taught to use the Infant/Toddler Environment Rating Scale or the Family Day Care Environment Rating Scale (Harms, Clifford & Cryer, 1989, 1990), and assessments were made of each child care site.

Interactional dynamics, the second strand of the DART Mentor Teacher Model, included infant/toddler development, the caregiver as curriculum, primary caregiving, creative problem-solving, and the relationship between the child and family. The social-emotional life of the infant/toddler, as defined in interactional processes, was identified and discussed in the context of physical and intellectual development. In addition, two specific seminars used video analysis, role-playing and modeling as sources for in-depth discussions.

Supervision, the third major strand of the training, was critical to the growth and development of competent caregivers. Good supervision is transformative and models the interactional qualities of signaling, reciprocity, attunement, synchrony and acknowledgement emphasized in this model (Restaino-Kelly A., &. Handler, J. 1996). Three seminars were allocated to identify the stages of developmental supervision to provide case examples, and to practice the specific steps of the mentoring process through role playing. Classes were held every other week, while a supervised field experience followed in the alternate week. Seminars were interactive and process oriented, and training strategies were designed to demonstrate how adults learn and to define "best practice" in early childhood education.

Course Outline

Seminars on the following topic areas included:

- Introduction to the DART Mentor Teacher Model
- Adult Development I, II
- Training to use the Harms-Clifford Environment Rating Scale
- Child Development
- Interactional Processes I, II
- The Caregiver as Curriculum
- Developing Primary Caregiver Systems
- Supervision and Mentoring I, II
- Developing Creativity and Problem-Solving Skills
- Promoting Effective Family Relationships
- Conducting Effective Staff Development Programs

Interactional Processes as the Theoretical Base

Interactional processes, such as signaling, reciprocity, attunement, synchrony, and acknowledgement, formed the theoretical base of the DART Mentor Teacher Model, (Escalona, 1967; Mahler, 1975; Stern, 1977,1985) and constituted its uniqueness. When practiced holistically, these processes created quality interactions between staff, adults and children and adults and families. In centers where children, as young as infants, are housed in groups for longer than eight hours, quality interactions are crucial to overall mental health. Therefore, it is critical that staff recognize the importance of quality interaction. In the DART Mentor Teacher Model, master trainers demonstrated these interactional processes through bi-weekly seminars, and in supervision sessions, field trainers (mentors) mirrored these processes. Supervisors also modeled them with their direct care staff, or in the case of family care providers, with their children and families.

Developmental Supervision and Mentoring

Traditionally, supervision has not been taught systematically in early childhood staff training programs. Though there are many positive and supportive supervisors in early childhood settings, many however are untrained The predominant mode for learning about supervision is on-the-job experience, with novices often mimicking the supervision styles which are modeled. Often teachers describe their supervision experiences as negative and judgmental. Many report that supervisors frequently approach the supervision process by telling them what they have done wrong and what they need to do, instead of engaging them in a collaborative, reflective, learning experience. This approach to training does not enable practitioners to grow professionally or to model "best practice." It may even deter growth. It also offers little opportunity for practical application and creates an unproductive relationship between the supervisor and the caregiver.

The developmental supervision method, identified for the DART Mentor Teacher Model, is an adaptation of a clinical supervision method, using interactional processes to promote collaboration and a non-judgmental approach (Cogan, 1973; Caruso & Fawcett, 1986; Glickman, 1990). In this process five steps are completed by each supervisor and practitioner.

The following steps outline the approach:

1. Preconference meeting

2. Observation

3. Analysis & Strategy

4. Supervision conference

5. Post-conference analysis

Field trainers (mentors) meet every other week with their site supervisor (protégé) to work through problem areas or weaknesses evident in their supervision, and to aid in implementing in-service staff development. It is the intention of the DART Mentor Teacher Model to provide child development content and communication skills, and to assist in the professional development of the supervisor, through focusing on the mentor/teacher relationship.

Lessons Learned

The DART Mentor Teacher Model was conceived primarily to provide in-service training opportunities to staff in infant/toddler centers and family child care settings who had little related training available. In the first two years of the model's implementation, the mentor/teacher component emerged as the most unique and strong feature. A one-to-one formal relationship between the supervisor (protégé) and the field trainer (mentor) was confirmed as the essential element of the program. The match between pairs was based on similar interests, problem solving skills and communication styles. Benchmarks of progress showed improvement in the areas of:

- communication skills.
- content dissemination.
- supervisor and staff interactions.
- self-confidence in supervision skills.

The strength of the relationship between mentor teacher, and less experienced teachers has promoted powerful changes and has provided support for novice teachers. In addition, the DART Mentor Teacher Model has offered opportunities for both supervisors and practitioners to gain clarity, initiate reflective practice, and engage in collegial mentoring.

The DART Mentor Teacher Model offers center and family child care supervisors and directors a means for professionalizing and "growing" staff (Jones, 1993). It supplies a content base, a structure for staff development, a supervisor and staff mentor model, and a way of supporting developmental (non-judgmental) supervision. Directors and supervisors shared their stories of growth and success while they participated in the DART Mentor Teacher Model. These accounts indicated that staff became more open to being supervised and mentored, and they felt more empowered. Staff were included in the training process in a more authentic way. Directors reported on "changed" lives, not only from their staffs' point of view, but from their own perspectives as well.

In ending this chapter, two vignettes are presented, one describes a director of a very large middle-income center in a suburban community, and the other profiles a director of a very small low-income center in a semi-urban community. The director of the large suburban program recounts her own fear and trepidation about bringing the DART Mentor Teacher Model to her staff. She was uncertain whether she could deliver this type of staff development authentically and effectively. She also recognized that it would require more work and effort on her part as a manager, especially as she struggled to stabilize and retain permanent staff. To her credit, her commitment and dedication to quality improvement supported her in promoting an effective staff development model. Despite her wavering confidence level, she improved staff practices and strengthened her own belief in the power and promise of staff development through supervision and mentoring. Through her involvement with the DART Mentor Teacher Project, this director realized that staff development is a never ending process. She also recognized that the struggle to provide quality is ongoing and that every small step toward professionalizing staff supported her own growth and development. In this manner, she embodied the spirit of the DART Mentor Teacher Model, which is dedicated to empowering and uplifting the professional and personal growth of both supervisor/director and practitioner.

In the second vignette, the director of a small semi-urban infant/toddler program, also a graduate of DART's Mentor Teacher Project, was initially a less enthusiastic participant. As a Child Development Associate credentialed teacher (CDA), she had a strong desire to retain and retrain staff, but she was more skeptical about the effectiveness of this staff training model. She had many barriers to overcome with staff. The most difficult obstacle was that while her staff was stable, it's members were more resistant to accepting a new style of staff development. They were entrenched in old habits, and new approaches to developmentally appropriate practices (DAP) were hard for them to embrace. Nonetheless, her desire to reshape her staff outweighed her own misgivings. Though she was not immediately successful in reaching her overall goal to professionalize her entire staff, she appreciated the importance of reaching one staff member at a time. She grew to understand that change comes in small increments over an extended period. Over the years, her intention to professionalize staff grows stronger and she continues to reach staff, one staff member at a time

Change in a director or supervisor directly influences staff and encourages them to grow professionally. Example and modeling by the supervisor or director are still the most effective means of changing staff behaviors. Therefore, as learned from the outcomes of the DART Mentor Teacher Project, mentoring provides one of the most powerful strategies for promoting professional development for child care staff. The following chapter provides a review of research on mentoring in the field of early care and education.

Activity 1

Exploring Barriers in Professionalizing Staff

Barriers	Very True in My Center	Somewhat True in My Center	Not True in My Center
1. Director who is not skilled in providing staff development opportunities			
2. Staff who have no desire to professionalize			
3. Staff who fear failure or change			
4. Lack of Time			
5. Lack of Funding			
6. Fill in your own			
7.			
8.			
9.			
10.			

Strategies for Overcoming Barriers

Review the chart above. Form committees in your center among people who are interested in furthering their professional development. Have each committee address one barrier and brainstorm some constructive, realistic strategies to overcome the problem. No problem is insurmountable if you work together to find creative solutions.

Activity 2

Breaking Ground:
a Staff Meeting Activity
for Team Building

Directors:

1) At your next staff meeting, ask staff to write down the first five words that come to mind when asked to describe the staff of your center.

2) Share answers. Include your own list.

3) Work together as a group to separate negative from positive responses.

4) Suggest that staff keep a teacher's journal to jot down specific incidents that illustrate the words they chose.

5) At the next gathering, share anecdotes. Find consensus on 5 things everyone feels proud of and 5 goals to improve within the next month.

6) Journals can help chronicle strategies for improvements and track successes.

7) Continue to share experiences and to set new goals for improvement at each staff meeting.

Understanding the Research

on Mentoring

Chapter 2

An experienced teacher is asked by her principal to mentor a colleague during her provisional year of teaching in kindergarten, although she has never received specific training for this task. She is asked to make sure that the new teacher conforms to the rules of the school and is oriented to school policies. No time is allotted for meetings, and it is implied that she will maintain a superior supervisory role during the mentoring process. As a highly competent and seasoned professional, she is excited about the positive aspects of sharing her knowledge. However, she is equally concerned about her administrator's expectations, and her own lack of training and time for this important responsibility.

This scenario represents one aspect of the emerging use of mentoring in the field of early childhood education. It also illustrates the dangers of implementing programs that fail to offer training and support for mentors. Ignoring a growing body of literature that documents effective mentoring models, this type of inappropriate practice is an issue of concern for professionals, who recognize the rich potential of mentoring in early childhood settings. It is the purpose of this chapter to examine research that will inform and guide professionals, who wish to deepen their understanding of the dimensions of mentoring and its appropriate applications.

What Is Mentoring?

Relationships are essential for development throughout life, and the essence of mentoring is being in a relationship (Buber, 1970). Daloz (1986) describes mentoring through the metaphor of a journey, which is a theme that dates back to Greek and Roman mythology. Homer's tale in the Odyssey introduces the character of Mentor, who was a guide, protector, and teacher selected by Odysseus to advise his young son, Telemachus. The modern concept of mentoring in early childhood has emerged from this literary tradition.

Contemporary literature on mentoring became popular during the 1970s in the fields of business and higher education. Research, in the areas of adult development and school reform, has also contributed to the current view of mentoring (Sheehy, 1976; Oja, 1980). Because of its diverse origins, no single unifying definition of mentoring is ascribed to in the research literature. Thus it is necessary to examine a range of perspectives to gain a global picture of its distinguishing features. Levinson, Darrow, Klein, Levinson & McKee (1978) and Zey (1984) describe a mentor as a guide, sponsor, or father figure, who oversees and promotes the career development of someone else through teaching and counseling.

These researchers focus on the role of mentoring for the purpose of improving productivity, reducing turnover, and strengthening corporate culture. A more humanistic and dynamic definition is provided by Anderson & Shannon (1988), who state that mentoring is:

> a nurturing process in which a more skilled or experienced person, serving as a role model, teaches, sponsors, encourages, counsels and befriends a less skilled or less experienced person for the purpose of promoting the latter's professional and/or personal development. Mentoring functions are carried out within the context of an ongoing, caring relationship between the mentor and protégé (40).

Because Anderson and Shannon emphasize mentor dispositions, such as sponsoring, encouraging and befriending, their definition fits well with the intensely interpersonal demands of the early childhood field. Mentoring functions, described by Anderson and Shannon, include observation and feedback, support meetings, and demonstration lessons that promote professional growth.

Expanding on these interpersonal dimensions, Gehrke (1988) portrays the mentoring relationship as one of gift giving, with development of wisdom as a way of seeing, shared between mentor and protégé. Parkay (1988) acknowledges the dynamic aspects of mentoring by describing it as a complex interactional relationship, which unfolds and changes over time. Focusing on change as the essential element, Mezirow (1991), Levinson (1978) and Daloz (1983; 1986) link mentoring to a transformational dimension, which can be characterized through the metaphors of a journey or a story. This view of mentoring emphasizes a deep and meaningful association between the mentor and protégé that is nonlinear and unconstrained by overly defined, unequal roles.

Mentoring Titles, Roles and Functions

Continuing the metaphor of a journey, Daloz (1983; 1986) describes a mentor as a trusted guide or leader, who steers the protégé through a professional sequence and challenges him/her to attain higher levels of development. Other designations for mentors include coach, positive role model, sponsor, master teacher, lead teacher, colleague teacher, peer teacher, and buddy (Schein, 1978; Bird, 1985; Hjornevik, 1986; Borko, 1986). Orienting to school procedures, collecting and disseminating information, providing data about teacher resources, offering advice to new teachers, and giving information about teaching strategies or the instructional process are listed as essential mentoring functions (Odell, 1986; Shulman & Colbert, 1988). In addition, structured problem solving activities, action research, self-observation and self-analysis emphasize the complex and multifaceted processes of reflection and change that are implicit in mentoring (Howey, 1985; Zimpher & Reiger, 1988).

Because the roles and functions of mentors are so diverse and change over time, some researchers have proposed conceptual models of the mentoring process. O'Neil (1981) outlines a model with six stages: entry, mutual building of trust, risk-taking, gaining teaching skills, developing professional standards, and dissolution of the mentoring relationship. Phillips (1977) and Kram (1983) make similar proposals. However, Phillips adds the dimension of transformation as a final phase, and Kram suggests redefinition as an end point. Gray and Gray (1985) describe a transactional relationship, based on a five step model, ranging from level one, in which the mentor plays the primary role, to level five, in which the protégé becomes a self-directed professional. In Gray and Gray's framework, the mentor functions as a situational leader, and the mentoring relationship enables the protégé to gain the competencies, confidence, realistic values and experience with which to function independently. This and other transformational views suggest the possibility of mentoring as an enduring partnership that changes to fit the needs of the participants over the life span. This perspective is congruent with the research on adult development.

Mentoring and Adult Development

Knowledge of adult development provides the foundation for building a sound mentoring program. In reviewing the large body of literature on this subject, the work of Erik Erikson, Carol Gilligan, Malcom Knowles, and Jack Mezirow emerges as the most applicable to adult development and mentoring in early childhood. Erikson's theory of psychosocial development (1950; 1963) proposes eight stages that extend across the life span. These are trust vs. mistrust, autonomy vs. shame and doubt, initiative vs. guilt, identify vs. role confusion, intimacy vs. isolation, generativity vs. stagnation, and ego integrity vs. despair. The psychosocial aspect of Erikson's theory is a key to understanding its relationship to mentoring. As the term psychosocial implies, an individual's social relationships have a major influence on the successful resolution of the crisis of change and movement from one stage to the next. Therefore, mentoring can provide valuable support to protégés in this regard. Erikson's stages of intimacy and generativity also offer opportunities for mentors to give back their accumulated wisdom and knowledge to individuals and society. Furthermore, the idea of nurturing the next generation promotes growth and satisfaction in both mentor and protégé (Gilligan, 1977; Noddings, 1984).

The work of Carol Gilligan (1977) delineates stages of adult development for women and extends Erikson's perspective. Gilligan describes an adult developmental progression with three levels. In the first level, the primary concern is for one's own well being. The second entails caring for others and self-sacrifice, and in the third the individual emerges as a legitimate person worthy of care and respect. Achievement of the third level leads to moral maturity, which involves a balance between caring for self and others. Gilligan's proposal has implications for mentoring. It is important for mentors to have achieved a relatively high level of maturity, in order to have the emotional and intellectual resources to provide protégés with appropriate support. It is also crucial for mentors to have enough understanding of adult development to be able to determine the needs of their protégés and respond appropriately.

In addition to Erikson and Gilligan, Malcolm Knowles (1980) is widely regarded as a leading authority on adult development. His research focuses on characteristics of adult learners and their learning styles. He believes that:

- adult self-concept is independent and self-directed,

- adults have an extensive bank of experiences for use as a learning resource,

- adults' readiness to learn is related to the developmental tasks of their social roles, and

- adults apply new knowledge immediately rather than in the future.

Therefore adults learn best by drawing on their own experience base, and they benefit from social contexts, such as mentoring, that enable them to become more autonomous.

Expanding on the views of Knowles, Jack Mezirow (1987) regards adult development as a process in which individuals reevaluate their experiences, and in so doing undergo transformations in their personal perspective. Mezirow describes these changes as transactional processes that can lead to profound reformulation of thought and action. Maturity is seen as a developmental process that cuts across the life span, and it includes development of autonomy, adaptation to life events and lasting changes in behavior. The views of Erikson, Gilligan, Knowles, and Mezirow are consistent with constructivism, which is a prominent philosophical position in early childhood education. Because there is a strong fit between mentoring and constructivism, it is crucial for mentors to have a working knowledge of this paradigm.

Constructivism

Constructivism is based on the belief that each individual, from birth, actively constructs knowledge. The process of constructivism involves individuals in an ongoing interaction or dialogue with the environment that continues throughout life (Erikson, 1963). It emphasizes personal construction of knowledge, as a dynamic and multifaceted process, through which the individual moves along a continuum toward autonomy and "progressively more adequate forms of cognitive and moral reasoning" (DeVries & Kohlberg, 1990,9).

Through processes of "seeing, searching, remembering, monitoring, correcting, validating and problem solving," individuals develop the metacognitive strategies necessary for independent and interpersonal functioning (Clay, 1991, 318). Constructivism is also based on social processes which include family, teachers and peers. Through meaningful interaction, individuals gain the social competence necessary for participation in a democratic society. Change is seen as beneficial and essential, and a mentoring relationship has the potential to provide the support system that mediates the risks and challenges inherent to this process.

Mezirow (1994) is a major contributor to the constructivist point of view, as it applies to adult development and mentoring. He regards "transformation as the central process in adult development which leads to a more inclusive, differentiated, permeable and integrated perspective" (155). He also proposes a ten phase process that enables a major transformation to occur. These phases are:

- Experiencing a disorienting dilemma.

- Undergoing self-examination.

- Conducting a critical assessment of internalized role assumptions and feeling a sense of alienation from traditional social expectations.

- Relating one's discontent to similar experiences of others or to public issues-recognizing that one's problem is shared and not exclusively a private matter.

- Exploring options for new ways of acting.

- Building competence and self-confidence in new roles.

- Planning a course of action.

- Acquiring knowledge and skills for implementing one's plans.

- Making provisional efforts to try new roles and to assess feedback.

- Reintegrating into society on the basis of conditions dictated by the new perspective (23).

In the transformational process, the adults' search for meaning allows for the realization of their identity and growth. Transformation, as described by Mezirow, causes disequilibrium, reformulation of self and professional identity, and adoption of new structures of making meaning. To facilitate transformation, a mentor may challenge the protégé and even force a situation of cognitive dissonance and reflection, which leads to a "new perspective and a new vision" (Daloz, 1986, 130).

A transformational model of mentoring, based on Mezirow's perspective, has the power to become a significant means for delivery of training and supervision in early childhood. In the earliest phase of the relationship, the essential unit of the mentoring process is the mentor and protégé dyad, which Parkay (1998) compared to the parent/child or teacher/pupil relationship. In this intimate context, the mentor serves as a facilitator, who is more knowledgeable and provides scaffolds, as the protégé constructs meaning that leads to higher levels of professional functioning (Mezirow, 1994). Later phases of the relationship allow for separation thereby promoting the protégé's independence.

The mentoring relationship provides an avenue of growth for the mentor as well as the protégé. Mentoring promotes positive identity and intimacy, and serves as a source of generativity. Stevens (1995) notes renewal and rejuvenation as rewards for mentors. Killian (1990) lists the additional benefits of recognition, enhancement of roles, and acquisition of new knowledge. Because mentors are asked to assume responsibilities as leaders and role models, their professional skills usually increase. Thus, mentoring also creates a new dimension in the early childhood leadership progression, which allows mentors, who are also teachers, to advance without moving out of the classroom (Henry & Phillips, 1997). In addition, mentoring promotes positive relationships with colleagues, which in turn foster establishment of bonds and make employees feel connected in ways that may increase morale and decrease staff turnover.

Effective Mentoring Programs in Early Childhood

In order to establish a positive and effective mentoring partnership, it is essential to provide training and support for mentors. All too often, as illustrated in the scenario at the beginning of this chapter, mentors are casually selected, inadequately trained and insufficiently compensated. The National Center for the Early Childhood Work Force has sponsored the development of an early childhood mentoring curriculum (Whitebook, Hnatiuk & Bellum, 1994). Research conducted by this group indicates that effective mentoring programs are:

responsive to the developmental needs of those they serve,

grounded in research on teacher and adult development,

supportive in nature, rather than linked to formal
evaluation processes,

forums for improving collegial connections between
mentors, protégés, employers, and trainers, and

learning systems that examine themselves, improve
how they function, and contribute to the collective
health of the early care and education community (126).

Other considerations, identified by this group, which must be weighed in the
design of mentoring programs, include: goals and purposes, type of program, developmental level of protégés, standards for entry and exit, content, structure and
rigor of professional standards, and processes of assessment.

Additional research on effective mentoring practices is emergent, but tenta-
tive conclusions may be drawn. Programs that provide formal, structured support,
in which a full time mentor is available to the protégé throughout the professional
development sequence, appear to be the most successful (Feiman-Nemsin & Parker,
1992). Mentors must have expertise in adult development, developmental supervision, reflective practice, developmentally appropriate practice, cognitive developmental theory and transformational theory (Martin, 1998). Adequate compensation,
through a reward system that offers release time and meaningful incentives, must
be provided to mentors. Also, careful screening of mentors' dispositions and their
areas of expertise are important to the quality of a program (Gillet & Halkett,
1988). Gray and Gray (1985) state that the best mentors are people-oriented and
secure, and they enjoy helping their protégés' gain confidence. It is also crucial for
mentors to be strong reflective practitioners, who are adept problem solvers and
communicators (Martin, 1998). In addition, Martin identifies the following 16
dimensions which are essential for development of a positive mentoring relationship. These are trust, openness, acceptance, comfort level, encouragement, support,

knowledge, expertise, reciprocity, mutuality, communication, feedback, reflection, empowerment, risk and vision.

Research indicates that mentoring shows great promise for use in induction programs for novice teachers. As they begin their journey of professional development, new teachers face obstacles, such as isolation, low salaries, lack of status, and limited opportunities for advancement (Huling-Austin, 1986). Without sufficient training and experience, beginning teachers tend to struggle with issues such as classroom management and discipline, student motivation, assessment, accommodation to children with specific individual needs, and parent involvement (Johnston & Ryan, 1983; Veeman, 1984). As they attempt to deal with these challenges, new teachers enter what Lilian Katz (1972) describes as the survival stage. According to Katz, this is followed by stages of consolidation, renewal and maturity, which are not always linear in their progression. Thus, beginning teachers' individual needs may vary. Well trained and experienced mentors can accommodate to their protégés' idiosyncratic patterns of development. Therefore, the need for further research that examines the effectiveness of mentoring models and training approaches is essential. The following chapter provides an account of one model of training, and it describes how the DART Mentor Teacher Model has been adapted in two child care programs for the purpose of mentoring novice teachers.

Activity 3

Applying Research to Practice

This chapter deals with the development of research about mentoring. The overall body of research cited here can be put on a continuum to show how current ideas about mentoring developed. You can break the research down into smaller, more usable pieces in order to see how it can best be applied to individual programs. Take the work of Carol Gilligan (23) for example:

Moral Maturity

I _____ I

Primary concern for   Caring for others   Balance between
ones own well being   Self sacrifice   self and others

Using the continuum as a guide, you can map out the first three phases in implementing a mentoring program.

First: (Concern for one's own well being)
Consider the needs of your staff. How will you identify the mentoring pairs? What's in it for them?

Second (Caring for others, self sacrifice)
How will the content of the mentoring relationships be determined? How will the center support the time the mentoring pairs need to spend?

Third: (Balance between self and others)
How will the dyads work together to enhance the quality of caring both deliver? How will the center benefit from this?

Plot your answers on the continuum below.
Share your goals and expectations for the program with staff.

I _____ I

Mentoring Initiatives:

Two Case Studies on Mentoring

Chapter 3

The DART Mentor Teacher Model provides center and family child care supervisors and directors with a new direction for professionalizing and "growing" staff (Jones, 1986, 1993). It also offers a content base, a structure for staff development, a supervisory and peer mentor model, and a means for conducting developmental supervision. As directors and supervisors, who have participated in the DART Mentor Teacher Model, share stories of growth and success, they describe staff who are more open to being supervised and mentored, and who are also empowered by this process. More importantly, they state that staff became a part of the professional development process in a more authentic way than ever before. Directors report on "changed lives," their own, as well as their staff.

In this chapter two agencies' experiences with mentoring are profiled to demonstrate contrasting applications of the DART Mentor Teacher Model. The first profile, by Florence Nelson, Ph.D., Executive Director of Summit Child Care Centers, documents her enthusiastic but cautious approach to implementing mentor training. Its content is taken from an article, "Profile of a Fledgling Mentor Teacher Program" (1995), in which she discussed her preparation and planning efforts leading to implementation of the model. The second profile by Suzanne Williamson, Regional Director of Monday Morning, Inc., a family child care agency, recounts a divergent approach taken to meet the needs of family child care providers. These two child care agencies' unique approaches to administering a mentor training model for staff are examined in this chapter.

Profile of a Fledgling Mentor Teacher Program

For Summit Child Care Centers (SCCC), a not-for-profit child care agency that enrolls 1200 children and employs a staff of 250, staff development is a high priority. SCCC's ongoing commitment to professional growth includes orientation programs, extensive on-site training, conferences, and tuition reimbursement for professional development activities. In New Jersey, as elsewhere, many child care workers have a minimal foundation in child development and early childhood education. Thus, emphasis on staff development at SCCC has been to develop the knowledge base of entry-level employees and to broaden and deepen the professionalism of experienced staff. Mentoring offered SCCC a means for promoting career development and fostering motivation for all staff to remain in the field.

In collaboration with the DART Center at Kean University, Summit Child Care Centers sponsored an on-site Mentor Teacher Training program, to enable experienced teachers to serve as mentors to those who were less experienced. The mentor training served three purposes. First, it extended the training resources available to teachers at SCCC by creating a network of trained mentors. Second, this training enhanced the professionalism of the mentors and gave them a step forward in their professional career track. Third, having a core of certified teachers, who were trained as mentors, allowed SCCC to attract provisional candidates for state teacher certification. In New Jersey, all graduates of four-year education programs must complete a year of teaching in a provisional status before receiving permanent certification. Many seek initial employment in a child care center that provides mentoring for full certification. The professional status of these individuals strengthens the overall credentials of SCCC staff.

The design of the Mentor Teacher Training Program at SCCC was influenced by a series of decisions which were made about how the program would be implemented in an on-site setting. These decisions and how they have shaped the mentor program are described. This information offers others guidance for developing a mentor/teacher training program and describes the process of implementing mentoring in a large multi-site agency.

Structure of the Mentor Program

The first step in establishing a mentoring program at SCCC was to provide on-site training for mentor-trainers, who were experienced teachers. This training occurred during twelve sessions conducted over a six-month period. It included group seminars and bi-weekly individual contact between the mentor-trainers and trainees, who were novice teachers at SCCC. It emphasized frequency and regularity of contact, with an emphasis on application of new strategies.

The training, which was designed and delivered by the Director of the DART Center, emphasized reflection, collegiality, and the importance of allowing time for people to change. In order for the mentor-trainers to share their reflections on the training process, sufficient time was allowed for discussion at each session. Mentor-trainers also kept a journal that was reviewed by the instructor after each session. To develop a sense of collegiality, the mentor-trainees had many opportunities for input into the design of the program during the early sessions. They also decided when and where the group would meet. The mentor-trainers set their own objectives and their own pace for establishing a relationship with their mentor-trainees.

Coordination with Center Directors

At the introductory session, several mentor-trainers were concerned that their center directors would not be supportive of the time required for them to work with their mentor-trainees. Dr. Nelson facilitated the training process for the mentor-trainers by helping center directors find ways to provide them with time away from their teaching responsibilities to attend sessions and to supply opportunities in the center for them to meet with their protégés. Also, center directors were oriented to the goals of the project, and were asked to provide input into the criteria for selection of mentor/trainers and mentor/trainees.

Content of the Training

The training for mentor-trainers had a dual focus: first, to build mentor-trainee relationships, and second to provide early childhood program content that would enhance all of the participants' understanding of child development and child care issues. The major goal of the content sessions was to bring all of the participants to a common standard of competence and to build their self-confidence in communicating on a professional level.

Mentor/Teacher Curriculum

The DART Mentor Teacher Model outlined 14 sessions to be conducted on a semester basis, so that the training would translate into a 3 credit undergraduate or graduate course on mentoring. The Director of Education of SCCC requested that the sessions be condensed from 14 to 12 in order to fit within SCCC's time schedule. The following course outline indicates the curriculum topics for each session.

Course Outline

1. Introduction to Mentoring: The Adult Learner

2. The Adult in the Mentoring Process:
   Mentor Principles, Roles and Functions

3. Mentoring: A Collaborative Approach to Supervision

4. Building Caring Relationships:
   Effective Supervision through Mentoring

5. Using Classroom Observation to Grow Teachers

6. Introduction to Techniques of Supervision and Feedback

7. Techniques of Supervision and Feedback: Communication Skills

8. Practice Skills: Classroom Organization

9. Practice Skills: Curriculum

10. Practice Skills: Lesson Planning

11. Practice Skills: Behavior Management

12. Review and Summary of Mentoring in Early Childhood

In addition to these topic areas, recommended resources for the training included:

- *Growing Teachers,* Elizabeth Jones (1993)

- *The Early Childhood Environment Rating Scale,*
  Harms, Clifford & Cryer, (1990)

- *The Infant/Toddler Environment Rating Scale,*
  Harms, Clifford & Cryer, (1989)

- *The Family Day Care Environment Rating Scale,*
  Harms, Clifford & Cryer, (1980)

Selection of Mentor-Trainers

Since the Mentor Teacher Training Program was an in-house initiative, SCCC was wary of setting criteria that would put mentor-trainees in competition with peers. Minimal criteria were set for participation, and the mentor-trainers were allowed to select their participants. A lengthy debate was held over whether to set minimal educational qualifications for mentor-trainers. This was a sensitive issue, because SCCC had teachers with many years of experience, who participated in on-site staff development programs. In order to avoid setting criteria that would exclude teachers, who lacked formal education/credentials, minimum requirements for participation were:

- at least three years of classroom experience and
- Lead Teacher status

Once the criteria for participants were set, a recruitment flyer, which described the DART Mentor Teacher Model, was sent to 45 eligible employees. Mentor-trainee candidates were invited to an introductory session. Twenty-five staff members, including their assistant directors, attended. After this session, applications were distributed. Fourteen people applied. Twelve were accepted and completed the training. The participating mentor-trainers had a range of 3-40 years of experience in the field. Some were early childhood certified, others had related degrees, and some had college credits in early childhood education.

Selection of the Protégés

Because of the size of SCCC's programs, it was possible to match mentor-trainers with protégés working in the same center. Proximity facilitated opportunities for these teams to have regular contact. In delineating criteria for choosing protégés from eligible staff, SCCC decided to involve the mentor-trainers in the selection process. The following criteria were set for protégé candidates:

- Less than two years with Summit Child Care Center, regardless of years in the field.
- Working with a similar age group as the mentor.
- Working at the same center as the mentor.
- Not working in the same classroom as the mentor.

Mentor-trainee selection was a three-step process. First the mentor-trainers gave the names of potential mentor-trainees to the Director of Education, and center directors were asked to approach these candidates about participation in the project. When trainees were identified, SCCC invited them to attend a joint meeting with mentor-trainers and trainees. At this meeting, goals and activities of the mentoring program were explained. The mentors and protégés had similar questions:

- What will the mentor/protégé teams actually do together?
- What will be my specific responsibilities?
- How are mentors and protégés teamed or paired?
- Will I be observed?
- Will I be videotaped?
- What if I don't feel comfortable being videotaped?
- How much time is required?
- How will I be able to take time away from my classroom in order to participate?
- How will participation benefit me?
- What if my mentor or protégé drops out of the project?
- Will there be rewards or recognition for participation?

At the culmination of this discussion, trainees applications were circulated. All of the candidates in attendance agreed to participate. At that joint meeting, trainer/trainee dyads learned how to conduct classroom observations using the Early Childhood Environment Rating Scale (ECERS) or the Infant/Toddler Environment Rating Scale (ITERS) (Harms, Clifford and Cryer, 1980, 1990). The trainer/trainee teams left the meeting with their first joint assignment which was to evaluate the trainee's classrooms using the ECERS or the ITERS.

Recognition and Compensation
for Mentors and Protégés

Questions of compensation and training were the most difficult challenges faced in the beginning of the Mentor Teacher Program at SCCC. Participants were offered the following in recognition of their participation:

1. Credit toward the 20 hours of training which is required annually for all Summit Child Care Center's staff. (Mentors accrued 30 training hours by the end of the project and protégés accrued 12-24 hours).

2. Release time from the classroom during work hours for teams to meet.

3. A certificate of completion issued by the DART Center.

4. Participating mentors, who were already certified teachers, were able to mentor provisional teaching candidates through the state of New Jersey's mentor teacher program. Mentors of provisional teaching candidates received a stipend of several hundred dollars for the school year, paid by the provisional teacher.

Sources of additional mentor compensation continue to be explored. Possibilities include salary adjustments upon satisfactory completion of training, stipends for mentoring new employees, and release time for consultation and planning. Possibilities for protégés include salary adjustments and eligibility for Lead Teacher status, which also includes a stipend.

This section described one application of the DART Mentor Teacher Model used by Summit Child Care Center, a very large multi-service agency. The remainder of this chapter is devoted to examination of an alternate approach, using similar objectives, but different methods of implementation.

Establishing a Mentor Program
for Family Child Care

Monday Morning, Inc. is a family child care management service. A private network of over 200 family child care providers are currently listed through Monday Morning in New Jersey. These providers have the benefit of a support service which includes insurance, equipment, technical assistance, and training. One of the most important mainstays of the support system is the personal contact between providers, office directors and staff. Regular on-site visits are also an important part of the program. These visits afford the self-employed providers an opportunity to share ideas, as well as gain insight and training from the provider director, and providers' review the high standards of quality care that Monday Morning has maintained since it's inception.

In keeping with a philosophy of support for providers, both within the Monday Morning network and in the field of family child care at large, it was natural to look at mentoring as an opportunity to enhance the quality of care. There was also a need at Monday Morning to create an opportunity for "Master Providers" to receive recognition for their valuable experience, and for them to share their knowledge with providers entering the field. Having worked with the DART Center's Training of Trainers Project for two years, it was natural for Monday Morning to establish a Mentor Teacher Training Program. The reasons for initiating a formal mentoring program at Monday Morning were:

- To offer experienced veteran providers a professional development opportunity to share their expertise, and gain increased recognition and compensation, resulting in retention in the field.

- To train and support new providers who need to renew interest and enhance program practice with children. Family child care studies have shown that providers learn best from other providers, such as mentors.

- To begin a program which could be duplicated throughout Monday Morning Moms Inc., nationwide, and enhance the current method of provider visits.

- To create a mentoring program which could be modified or adapted for use by the family child care profession.

In New Jersey there are over 4,000 family child care providers who voluntarily register with the state, and an estimated additional 12,000 unregistered providers who also work in their homes caring for children. In response to a 1994 survey, compiled by the Family Day Care Organization of New Jersey, providers confirmed that they would stay in the field longer with increased compensation and recognition, and would seek training when it was offered. This group of respondents also stated that low earnings and long hours were among their main reasons for possibly leaving their careers. They listed isolation, limited adult interaction, and lack of training for working with mixed age groups as their most significant concerns. Monday Morning felt that a strong mentor relationship would address these concerns and meet the needs of both mentors and protégés.

Putting It Together

Initiation of a mentor/teacher program at Monday Morning raised important questions.

How do you set up a mentor program for caregivers who work independently in their homes?

How do you offer training that does not take staff away from the children during the normal workday?

How do you make sure that this training is relevant to settings with mixed-age groups for a single caregiver who works long hours?

Monday Morning believed the DART Mentor Teacher Model addressed the issues raised in these questions.

Formal Organization of the Program

In organizing the program, the Monday Morning Provider Advisory Committee was a valuable resource. Several of the committee members responded to an initial announcement about the proposed mentor program. Others offered insights into the barriers that would prohibit them from participation. Discussion included what course content would be most relevant. It also addressed anxieties associated with being a mentor, as well as concerns about parents' responses and arranging time away from the family day care home. Training sessions were held from 9:00-1:00 P.M. on five Saturday mornings from February through May, 1995. Arrangements were made to use a central location, which was the Kean University Child Care Center. Class content included:

- Introduction to mentoring the adult learner and training in the use of the Harms/Clifford Environment Rating Scales.

- Communications, interactional processes, and developmental supervision.

- Caregiver as curriculum.

- Creativity and problem solving.

- Family relationships.

- Review and summary of mentoring principles.

Resources for conducting the training matched those used in the pilot project of Summit Child Care Center. They included: Growing Teachers and Teaching Adults by Elizabeth Jones, (1993, 1986) and the Family Day Care Environment Rating Scale by Thelma Harms, Deborah Cryer, & Richard M. Clifford (1989). Additional readings were taken from various articles in Young Children the journal of the National Association for the Education of Young Children, (NAEYC), Zero to Three publications from the National Center for Clinical Infant Programs, and other related reprints and video's. Each active provider in the Monday Morning network was also given the Creative Curriculum for Family Child Care by Diane

Trister Dodge and Laura J. Colker (1992). Course content included methods of using these materials with protégés. As an additional resource, the extensive Monday Morning Library was brought to each class.

The schedule for the four-month program also included mentor "field visits." Mentors worked with their protégés in their homes at least four times in between seminars. A fifth visit included working together at the mentor's worksite, so the beginning caregiver could see the child care environment first hand and observe the interactions of an established family child care home. In addition, the Family Day Care Environment Rating Scale was completed by both mentors and protégés, to form a common ground for setting goals. Mentors also kept an ongoing journal of the experience. As a final component, the directors of all Monday Morning offices volunteered to attend as many workshops as possible to be fully knowledge-able of the program. Video's of each workshop were also available to any provider in the network.

Mentor Selection and the Matching Process

Mentor candidates were chosen according to standards set by the DART Mentor Teacher Model. Requirements for selection included three years of experi-ence in child care. Educational background was considered in candidate selection. Candidates were chosen from those who demonstrated leadership and communica-tion skills and a willingness to work closely with a beginning provider over the months of training. A commitment to the completion of all phases of the program and to the Monday Morning, Inc. philosophy was expected. A written application was submitted by each mentor candidate.

Mentors were chosen from those who volunteered or were nominated. It was made clear to both the mentors and protégés that the goal of this project was to enhance the quality of care and to offer providers, who were entering the field, more in-depth support. Mentors were matched with protégés by geographical location. An effort was also made to arrange partnerships in which personalities would be compatible.

Creating the Partnership, the Crucial Support of Parents and Providers Working Together

One of the major concerns of mentors was how "their parents" would feel about them leaving the children in the care of a substitute while they worked with their protégé. One of the strongest benefits of choosing a family child care situation is that the children and their families can form a strong relationship with a single caregiver. Monday Morning providers are very sensitive to this bond with families and are proud of the quality of care they offer based on this triad. Knowing that communication would be the most important solution to this concern, the following steps were taken:

- An announcement was sent from the Program Coordinator to the parents in each mentor's home, notifying them that their provider had been chosen to participate in this very special project.

- Each mentor received a full description of the project and was encouraged to share it with parents.

- Each mentor arranged a special meeting for parents if they did not know the substitute.

These strategies, coupled with the mentors enthusiasm, resulted in a successful experience.

Beyond Warm Fuzzies

A review of the Mentor Teacher Training Program would be incomplete without discussing the rewards of participation. A program information sheet developed by Monday Morning describes benefits.

"Many experienced providers seek new challenges beyond their family child care homes, and already informally mentor new providers. Learning to be a mentor involves a process of self examination that would enhance the mentor's professional development. Skills learned in this workshop will benefit the provider who plans to expand into training and/or advocacy, earn a CDA credential, continue college, or commence a graduate degree.

The mentor training project will accrue 20 hours of training credit, many of which can be used towards the Child Development Associate Credential (CDA). Along with the professional recognition, mentors will receive a stipend for all planned site visits with their protégé to cover the cost of a substitute and transportation."

Where from Here? Evaluating the Program

To date, the Mentor Teacher Training Program appears to be successful. Mentors have reported that the experience has been meaningful for both themselves and their protégés. Results from the Family Day Care Environment Rating Scale (1989) have shown improvements in the areas of language, interaction and curriculum. Mentors view their role as a new career path in their professional development progression. Monday Morning, Inc. has decided to continue to assign mentors to each new caregiver. Follow-up seminars are planned, and the program will be reviewed for inclusion in Monday Morning Moms Inc. nationwide. The Program Coordinator continues to work with the DART Center to refine the program.

These two applications of the DART Mentor Teacher Model represent the range of possibilities for inclusion of mentoring in staff development efforts. Though the goals are similar, it is important to note the diversity within the delivery systems. Accounts of these two training approaches can provide information to those who are involved with the development of mentoring programs for differing types of centers. It is also productive to understand the process undertaken by both agencies to address the barriers within their organizations. The next chapter addresses the barriers involved in child care center accreditation and highlights the role of mentor/teacher consultants as key figures in the process of accreditation.

Activity 4

Survey for Potential Protégés

1. Why are you interested in entering into a mentoring relationship?

    _____

2. List three of your goals.

    _____

    _____

    _____

3. What are the characteristics you are looking for in a mentor?

    _____

    Will you be more comfortable with an older or younger person?
    Someone who works in your room or elsewhere?
    A peer or a supervisor?

    _____

4. How will you know you have met your goals? What assessments can you look for?

    _____

5. Think about a teacher you had in your life who made a lasting impression on you. What qualities did you most admire about her?

    _____

6. How much time do you have to give to the mentoring relationship? When can you meet with your mentor?

    _____

Survey for Potential Mentors

1. Why are you interested in entering into a mentoring relationship?

2. What are three of your goals for the program?

   _____

   _____

   _____

   What do you hope to gain?

   _____

3. What kind of person are you interested in mentoring?
   A new employee? A young person? Someone who has been on
   staff but has little formal training?

   _____

4. How will you know your protégé has met her goals?

   _____

   What kinds of changes will you be looking for?

   _____

5. How would you describe yourself as a caregiver?

   _____

   What are your greatest strengths? Where can you improve?

   _____

6. How and when will you meet? What would be the ideal structure
   of the relationship for you?

   _____

   _____

Applying a Mentor/Teacher Consultant Model

to the Accreditation Process

Chapter 4

T he final report of the New Jersey Department of Human Services (DHS) Ad Hoc Early Childhood Accreditation Work Group (April, 1998) states:

> New Jersey is among a number of states throughout the nation that are exploring how best to stimulate improvements in the quality of the programs offered to young children by means of accreditation incentives. The national level is no less active. The increasing demand for quality in early care and education and the widening variety of program suppliers must strive to improve the characteristics that typify quality programming for children. Accreditation is one way among many that can have dramatic effects on young children, their parents, the professionals that operate programs and the nation at large

The recommendations in this report confirm the importance of accreditation in the quest for high quality child care. This report also provides support for the accreditation of child care centers through the provision of funds for application and validation fees, improvement of programs to meet professional standards, and the employment of support personnel to facilitate the accreditation process.

The DHS Ad Hoc report cites the barriers identified by program directors, which delay or undermine their progress in attainment of accreditation. Among the identified barriers, financial need is primary to most programs. This area encompasses cost of the application and validation fees, additional expenses for equipment and materials, and any unfunded expenses needed for program improvement, including staff development, technical assistance, or building renovations. Other important barriers cited are boards of directors, staff members and providers, and parents.

An additional report, issued in July, 1998 by the Professional Development Committee of the New Jersey Child Care Advisory Council (CCAC), addresses aspects of accreditation. The report, entitled "Indicators of Quality in Early Care and Education: An Issue Paper," defines quality according to the literature in early care and education. Based on the work of leaders such as John Dewey, Jean Piaget, Barbara Biber, Susan Isaacs, T. B. Brazelton and Daniel Stern, the report identifies key indicators that constitute high standards of quality. The following quote taken from this report, documents the content of the report and how it fits well with Developmentally Appropriate Practice (DAP). It states:

> ".....children are active learners who thrive through positive
> engagement with people and materials, having the freedom
> to play, to explore, to problem-solve and to reason. Children
> learn best in an environment that is suitable to their mode
> of learning and their developmental abilities, and when the
> adults involved are responsive to individual as well as group
> needs" (Introduction, 1).

Because the quality of early childhood programs makes a difference in the lives of children, their families and ultimately society as a whole, it is imperative to attend to the key indicators outlined in the report. These indicators are: Leadership Characteristics, Teacher/Caregiver Behaviors, Parent and Caregiver Relationships, Curriculum, Environment, and Resources for Quality Programs. The move to accredit programs involves meeting standards established in these key indicators.

It is important to note that the recommendations in the reports from the NJ Department of Human Services (DHS) Ad Hoc Committee on Accreditation and the Professional Development Committee of the New Jersey Child Care Advisory Council go beyond recognition of the role of financial assistance for accreditation and identify the provision of support personnel as an additional essential component. This chapter examines the steps that are required to take a child care center, family day care home, or school age program through accreditation, and it makes a case for the role of a mentor/teacher consultant, as an integral figure in this process.

The DHS Ad Hoc Committee report lists the steps in the accreditation process, which need to occur in order for assessment to be carried out. Some of these steps include completing the accreditation application, conducting a readiness survey and supervising a developmental evaluation process which includes: self-study, program improvement, rating staff and environment, and recommendations for an evaluation visit. The full process of accreditation is rigorous and complex, and there are a growing number of professional organizations that are involved in the process. There are five national accrediting bodies in early care and education that grant their own accreditation. These organizations are:

- National Early Childhood Professional Accreditation (NECPA) which is linked to the National Child Care Association

- National Academy of Early Childhood Programs (NAECP), an arm of the National Association for the Education of Young Children

- National Association for Family Child Care

- Council on Accreditation of Services to Families and Children (COA)

- National School Age Child Care Alliance.

Obtaining accreditation from one of these organizations requires a strong commitment from child care center boards, administration, staff and parents. The barriers addressed in the DHS Ad Hoc Committee report which include time, cost, directors demand for resources, staff, as well as parent and administrative involvement, often overwhelm even the most committed program directors. In New Jersey, only 159 of the over 3,400 licensed child care centers are accredited by one of these national associations.

Mentoring Activities to Assist in the Accreditation Process

Directors who are beginning the accreditation process have many questions about the starting point. Questions about the completion of the application for accreditation alone may cause directors to delay the process. A mentor/teacher consultant helps the director understand the application, the readiness survey and the outline or plan for moving the center through the accreditation process. The mentor/teacher consultant asks, "What does the center need in order to get through an accreditation process, in the areas of environment, curriculum, planning, and quality of language and interactions?" To answer this question, she may spend time in classrooms and view these rooms as an accreditation validator might observe them.

She also outlines and explains the steps of the accreditation process. These include:

1. Review accreditation manual and application process with director.
2. Review and conduct readiness survey.
3. Conduct self-assessment review (What do we need to begin?).
4. Assist director in developing a timeline.
5. Conduct staff development needs & analysis.
6. Conduct environment observations.
7. Provide workshops with individual and full group staff.
8. Provide director support to improve policies and procedures.
9. Provide parent/board training.
10. Review final program.

Building a Team

The mentor/teacher consultant not only provides technical assistance to child care centers seeking accreditation but also functions as a team builder. While the director manages daily operations and the overall program, the mentor/teacher consultant can identify staff members, who can serve on a team that promotes the goals of accreditation. As a team, staff members can be charged with the task of:

- overseeing environmental standards.

- assessing curriculum quality and developmentally appropriate practices (DAP).

- promoting health and safety standards.

- assessing program management.

The tasks involved in program accreditation may seem overwhelming, but when shared among staff members, they become more manageable. Staff are more apt to address issues of quality favorably when acting as a team in collaboration with a mentor/teacher consultant.

In pursuit of team building activities, a mentor/teacher consultant can identify staff who will work with others to:

- evaluate classrooms using the Early Childhood Environment Rating Scale (ECERS) or the Infant/Toddler Environment Rating Scale (ITERS) (Harms, Clifford & Cryer, 1989, 1990)

- train staff in developmentally appropriate practices (DAP)

- train staff in talking about their programs in order to convey their understanding of developmentally appropriate practices (DAP) to validators

In addition, staff team members need opportunities to meet regularly to discuss issues raised in the accreditation process. A mentor/teacher consultant can lead sessions on topics such as program management, curriculum, and quality interactions. The specific contributions of a mentor/teacher consultant are described in the following sections.

In 1994, the DART Center's major founders, The Schumann Fund for New Jersey and the Victoria Foundation, subsequently joined by the Prudential Foundation, came together to sponsor a collaborative training project based on the needs of child care centers to:

- improve staff quality through literacy and child development training.
- upgrade center quality through NAEYC accreditation efforts.

This project, a joint initiative between the DART Center at Kean University and the Life Skills Center at Montclair State University, combined the DART Mentor Teacher Model and a Life Skills CDA training program from Montclair State University. It focused on three components: a literacy-based Child Development Associate training (CDA), a supervisory mentor/teacher training of 20 educational staff, and support and assistance training toward NAEYC accreditation for these centers. This joint-initiative emphasized mentoring for staff development. A literacy based child development curriculum, described in *Building Literacy Through Child Development* (Restaino-Kelly & Barbell Rudolph, 1997), comprised the training component.

The program was called the Kean University/Montclair State University Collaborative for Child Care Training in New Jersey. A mentor/teacher consultant was chosen from an accredited urban center to mentor five of the twenty centers in the project. These five centers were working toward NAEYC center accreditation. The mentor/teacher consultant met representatives from the five centers as a total group, then as a small group and individually. She provided technical assistance and met on-site to observe the quality of each center's environment.

After an initial assessment the mentor/teacher consultant prepared a report for the center director, identifying the status of the environment, curriculum, and staff interactions, and including recommendations for completing the readiness survey. Of the five center directors the mentor/teacher consultant worked with, one was in the process of reapplying for accreditation, three were beginning t heir readiness survey, and one decided that her center was not yet ready to apply for accreditation.

In an informal survey of center directors who had been through the accreditation process, the following areas were identified as most important to the accreditation support process.

1. Director Training

Director training was deemed to be the most important by all the directors surveyed. Directors agreed that an overall review of the accreditation process and a timeline of steps to be taken were crucial. Directors were provided emotional support through assistance from the mentor/teacher consultant, and they benefited from conversations in which they could express their concerns, fears and questions regarding the accreditation process.

2. Staff Training in DAP Specific to Each Age Group

Directors and staff identified developmentally appropriate practice (DAP) as the most needed area of training for staff and administrators. They agreed that all center personnel must be able to articulate DAP in order to demonstrate a sound developmental program. The mentor/teacher consultant was able to provide staff development opportunities. She also offered team building activities and identified potential leaders or peer mentors, who could assist others in the process of improving environment, curriculum and interactions.

3. Staff Training in Observation and Evaluation

Directors and staff concurred that all center personnel needed training in observation and classroom assessment, as well as opportunities to reflect on and to discuss their own practice. Training appropriate to their needs was conducted by the mentor/teacher consultant in the overall use of the Harms/Clifford Environment Rating Scale for infant/toddler and preschool settings. Once staff were able to more objectively view themselves and their classroom environment, they began the process of improving program quality and addressing their own needs.

4. *Team Approach to Observation and Evaluation*

Independent evaluation of individual classrooms was not as helpful to center staff as was the process of evaluation of classrooms as a team, with a staff member from a different class observing and assessing the environment. Each staff member was paired with a colleague to observe each other's classroom and to provide feedback.

5. *Teach Staff How to Talk about Your Program to Convey Developmentally Appropriate Practicer DAP*

Directors concurred that it was essential for staff to understand their centers' operational policies. Therefore, staff were prepared to answer questions about appropriate practice and philosophy. The mentor/teacher consultant assisted in this preparation by discussing staff members' questions about practice.

6. *Conduct a Pre-Accreditation Visit*

The mentor/teacher consultant served a key function in moving the centers toward accreditation while freeing the center directors and providing for staff and program needs. This consultant offered the psychological and emotional support to center directors and staff throughout the rigorous process of preparation for the accreditation assessment. One month prior to an accreditation visit, directors indicated that it was valuable to schedule a pre-assessment consultation with a mentor/teacher consultant or a practice visit. Staff and administration benefited from the objective advice and technical assistance, offered by the mentor/teacher consultant prior to the actual validation visit.

Program directors, who participated in this process, agreed that they achieved a better understanding about the procedures needed to attain accreditation when they had a mentor/teacher consultant to assist them. They recognized the serious nature of the accreditation process. For many centers, the lack of time to accomplish goals and improve classroom practice makes accreditation a difficult process. A director is immersed in daily responsibilities and may be unclear about how to carry out the tasks necessary to reach accreditation. Time and support are critical in making change happen. Although change is often a slow, step by step process, the improvement in the quality of care makes accreditation of child care centers worth the effort. A mentor/teacher consultant can assist in bringing this process to fruition.

The following chapter describes a mentoring model for graduate students in an early childhood Master of Arts program, which is partially based on the DART Mentor Teacher Model. Use of alumni mentors distinguishes the model. Portfolios, documentation, and book arts are integrated as strategies for supporting students' professional development.

Activity 5

Conducting Your Own Research

1. Review the bibliography appended to this text. How many of the books listed are you familiar with? Do you have a professional development library at your center? What resources would be necessary to start one? Why would you consider this a priority?

2. Gain access to the World Wide Web. If you cannot do this at your center, go to your local library or Internet CafÈ. Go to a search engine and do a general search on mentoring in early childhood programs. Attached is a sample of what you might see. Any of these articles can be instantly accessible to you!

3. What are some other ways to find resources to broaden your knowledge of mentoring and other important issues?

Suggested Internet Resources for Childcare Providers

1. Childcare Providers and Parents:
   www.open.org/zepedaf/

2. Childcare Parent/Provider Information Network:
   www.childcare-ppin.com

3. Resources for Childcare Providers:
   www.kcels.org/webkids/cheresour.html

4. ABC's of Safe and Healthy Childcare:
   www.cdc.gov/ncidad/hip/abc/abchtm

Your search for **"mentoring in early childhood"** resulted in:
11 Reviewed Web Site Topics
32,355,459 Web Search Results

New search   or   Search within results

Reviewed Web Site Topics

Jump to: Web Search Results   -   Search Box

Education >

- **Early childhood & preschool** >
    - Early childhood development
    - Early childhood & preschool associations
    - Early childhood & preschool parent resources
  - **Activities** >
    - Learning activities for early childhood & preschool
    - Stories for early childhood & preschool
    - Music for early childhood & preschool
- **Education research** > Early childhood education research

Web Search Results

Jump to: Reviewed Web Site Topics   -   Search Box

RESULTS 1 - 10 of 32,355,459 total results grouped by site

HIDE SUMMARIES | ···UNGROUP THESE RESULTS | Next 10

Classifieds:
Find anything from concert tickets to computers, poodles to personals

Application Form
A resume, or brief summary of your work experience relevant to child care, must accompany this application. If it is not clear from your resume, please include a very brief description of the program ...
77% **Date: 26 Jul 1998**, Size 6.5K,
http://ericps.ed.uiuc.edu/ccdece/seminar/semappl.html
···Grouped results from http://ericps.ed.uiuc.edu/ccdece/seminar/semappl.html

Two Prestigious Awards for Book on How Young Children Learn
October 1998 Winner of an Early Childhood News Directors' Choice Award earlier this year, the book, , has just added another accolade: A Parent's Guide Award. The winners of the Early Childhood News Directors' Choice Awards were selected by a panel of six judges whose combined ...
77% **Date: 27 Oct 1998**, Size 6.5K, http://bookflash.com/releases/100078.html

Play And Early Childhood Development by Johnson, James E. // Joint Author: Christie, James ...

Play And Early Childhood Development by Johnson, James E. // Joint Author: Christie, James F. // Joint Author: Yawkey, Thomas D. ISBN 032101166X BOOK TOPICS COMPANY INFO SEARCH COMMENT ON A BOOK MOTIVATIONAL PRODUCTS Copyright © ...
76% **Date: 16 Oct 1998**, Size 11.8K, http://www.opengroup.com/open/eabooks/032/032101166X.shtml
···Grouped results from http://www.opengroup.com/open/eabooks/032/032101166X.shtml

The Center for Early Childhood Leadership Home Page

The Center for Early Childhood Leadership is dedicated to enhancing the management skills, professional orientation, and leadership capacity of early childhood educators. To find out more about who we are, what we do, and how we might serve you and your organization, spend some time exploring our web site. ...
74% **Date: 13 Oct 1998**, Size 6.4K, http://nlu.nl.edu/cecl/

Early Success in School Through Parent Involvement makes for Smart Kids., preschool, ...

Assist your baby using these secrets and tips to assure early success for your child in school. Dr. and Mrs. Falkenstein reveal techniques that show how to achieve educational success.
73% **Date: 18 Aug 1998**, Size 6.8K, http://www.i-netmall.com/shops/smartkids/

Educational Learning Materials and Activities - DLM Early Childhood Program

childrens' learning materials as well as educator and parenting resources
73% **Date: 12 Oct 1998**, Size 4.3K, http://www.mhlm.com/

Updated on October 29, 1998 INDIAN BOOKS CENTRE PHILOSOPHY AND RELIGION : Hinduism, ...

Updated on October 29, 1998 INDIAN BOOKS CENTRE PHILOSOPHY AND RELIGION : Hinduism, Buddhism, Jainism, Islam, Comparative Studies Ancient Buddhist Monasteries: India And Nepal/S Gajrani ISBN: 81-85163-91-X US$30 Banaras Sarnath ISBN: 81-7436-051-4 US$22.80 ...
73% **Date: 29 Oct 1998**, Size 79.7K, http://www.ibcindia.com/october98.htm

A Cause For Students And Retirees To Do Specific Volunteering That Pertains To Your Major, ...

A Cause For Students And Retirees To Do Specific Volunteering That Pertains To Your Major, Or Past Profession. Do It Now.
73% **Date: 17 Oct 1998**, Size 46.2K, http://www.volunteersmarter.org/step5.htm
···Grouped results from http://www.volunteersmarter.org/step5.htm

SOURCES & SIDEBARS FOR FRIDAY, OCT. 9: HEAD START BILL GOES TO WHITE HOUSE

Legislation to approve spending for Head Start and extend a program to help low-income families is now before President Clinton. The measure authorizes $35 ...
73% **Date: 10 Oct 1998**, Size 8.7K, http://www.pathfinder.com/money/latest/press/PW/1998Oct09/360.html
···Grouped results from http://www.pathfinder.com/money/latest/press/PW/1998Oct09/360.html

Parent Information and Resource Center

Trainings and Workshops. Conference Name Location Date Contact information Sponsored by Quality Infant and Toddler Caregiving Workshop Sheraton University Hotel and Conference

Center, Syracuse, NY June ...
71% **Date: 6 Aug 1998**, Size 18.6K, http://www.nwrel.org/pirc/workshops.html

RESULTS 1 - 10 of 32,355,459 total results   **HIDE SUMMARIES** | ***UNGROUP THESE RESULTS**
grouped by site   **| Next 10**

Search Box   Jump to: **Reviewed Web Site Topics** - **Web Search Results**

People Finder - Shareware - Dictionary - Thesaurus - Company Capsules - More...

| | | Search Tips | **FIND** exactly |
| New search | or   Search within results | Advanced Search | what you **WANT** |

Mentoring in an Early Childhood

Master of Arts Program

Chapter 5

This chapter describes the evolution of a mentoring program for Masters of Arts candidates in the Department of Early Childhood and Family Studies at Kean University in New Jersey. It provides a detailed account of the graduate coordinator's ongoing efforts to devise a plan for mentoring, which assists students in completing their program of studies and engages them in transformative processes that support personal and professional development and change. It also demonstrates how the fundamental principles of the DART Mentor Teacher Model can be adapted to an advanced early childhood program.

A Rationale for Mentoring

In her first semester as the graduate coordinator of the Master of Arts program in the Department Early Childhood and Family Studies at Kean University, one of Dr. Ashelman's first points of contact with seven students was to inform them that they had failed the comprehensive examination. Although she agreed with each of the three readers of the examinations, this troubling situation prompted questions: How had these students been able to progress so far in their program of studies without the skills to adequately complete this important requirement successfully? Had these students received appropriate assistance as they prepared for the comprehensive examination? How could the support system provided by the department be strengthened? How could the graduate coordinator structure her role, so she could sustain students' personal and professional growth and maintain the standards of the department? Mentoring appeared to provide a partial answer.

As she began to explore mentoring through reading and discussions with colleagues, the graduate coordinator realized she was not alone in her search for how to better meet the needs of her students. The climate of isolation, competition, and individualism frequently found in graduate school is a time honored tradition that can "render nurture virtually impossible" (Kerr, 1993, 10). Early childhood education is a nurturing profession, however, that should favor the formation of warm, caring relationships and the development of cooperative interpersonal skills. She experienced this type of interaction as a master's student in a Family and Child Development Department, and she hoped to emulate it in her position as graduate coordinator.

Mentoring Redefined

The graduate coordinator's goal for applying mentoring in the early childhood master's program at Kean University forced her to reexamine her understanding of the mentoring process. She was aware of mentoring partnerships that featured dyads of mentor and protégé. However, she wondered whether there were alternative configurations. Could she be considered a mentor in her role as graduate coordinator, and could groups of students working together constitute a mentoring relationship?

The concept of mentoring that helped answer these questions and had the most relevance for guiding her work came from *Breaking the circle of one: Redefining mentorship in the lives and writing of educators* (1997). The authors of this book acknowledge the traditional definition of mentoring, which depicts the mentor as a wise and knowledgeable person, who undertakes a special commitment to counsel, teach, and advise a less experienced person. In addition, the dyad of mentor and protégé are described as a "mentoring circle of two," in which both partners develop a deep and extended relationship (Hughey, 1997, 101). The mentoring process is also expanded to include a "circle of one-to-many" or "many-to-one," (Hughey, 1997, 103). Seen in this light, mentoring includes a greater number of participants, and it creates a context in which all parties learn from each other and promote change. Thus, a mentoring group can facilitate personal and professional growth, with the roles of mentor and protégé shared among its members. At its best, mentoring is reciprocal, mutualistic, transactional, and multilevel (Stansell, 1997). All of these aspects can be enhanced by enlarging the circle of participants in the mentoring relationship.

Further refining the concept of mentoring at the graduate level, Cox (1997) notes that a mentor should serve as a "sounding board," who offers multiple points of view, and the protégé should have "the freedom to use, adapt, or discard the mentor's advice at all times" (84). This construct is particularly appropriate for master's students in early childhood education, a field that must foster respect for individual differences, facilitate development of autonomy, and provide support for advocates who question inappropriate practice. In addition, mentors must be intrinsically motivated to invest something of themselves in an effort to develop their protégés' sense of belonging to the profession of teaching (Stansell, 1997). This view of mentoring fits well with Mezirow's paradigm of transformational learning described in Chapter Two. Defined in this manner, mentoring also serves to help undergird the goals and purposes of the Early Childhood and Family Studies Department at Kean University. The following section describes the master's program and the rationale for providing mentoring for its students.

The Early Childhood and Family Studies' Master of Arts Program at Kean University

The Master of Arts program in the Department of Early Childhood and Family Studies includes the study of children, from the prenatal period through the age of eight, as well as their families. The program is designed to meet the needs of the diverse urban and suburban population that Kean University serves. Enrollment is open to early childhood and family studies professionals, who wish to strengthen their background in areas such as teaching, administration and family life education, and to individuals who are preparing to enter the field.

The master's program offers four options for specialization. These are Advanced Curriculum and Teaching, Administration in Early Childhood Settings, Education for Family Living, and Classroom Instruction, an initial certification program, which is pending approval. Students in the first three options complete 33 credits, including 27 semester hours of required and elective courses. The Classroom Instruction Option requires completion of 42 credits, including a six semester hour student teaching experience. A field-based Advanced Seminar research project is required and is usually carried out during the last two semesters of matriculation. Successful completion of a comprehensive examination and preparation of a professional portfolio are also mandatory.

The Master of Arts program in the Department of Early Childhood and Family Studies is based on the tenets of developmental theory, with an emphasis on constructivism (DeVries & Kohlberg, 1990). Learning and development are considered to be continuous processes, beginning at birth and extending throughout the life span. The faculty of the department share a commitment to facilitation of students' construction of the knowledge, skills and values, which are necessary to function creatively and productively in diverse early childhood settings. The master's program is also designed to increase the professional competencies of students, so they will be able to:

1. employ effective communication skills when working with children, families, colleagues, and the larger community.

2. understand the concept of collaboration and use it effectively with colleagues, families, and other educational stakeholders.

3. critically analyze leadership and teaching skills and apply them to present and future practice.

4. participate in the processes of self and shared assessment for the purpose of developing a professional portfolio, that is congruent with appropriate practice for young children and is supportive of the dynamic processes of change.

5. engage in research that contributes to professional growth, enhancement of classroom practice, and the quality of education and care for children and families.

6. participate in organizations that promote advocacy for young children and their families and provide opportunities for leadership.

7. develop a personal/professional philosophy and code of ethics which guides practice.

Achievement of all of these goals can be enhanced through mentoring.

The Master of Arts program at Kean University serves an important function in New Jersey. It is the only true early childhood program in the state, and it has been recognized for its diverse options of curriculum, administration, family studies and certification (NAEYC, 1992). The coordinator functions as the advisor for the entire population of approximately fifty-five students.

The master's students in the department fit into three broad categories, which include recent recipients of bachelor's degrees in early childhood education or child development, mature practitioners, who have been out of school for as many as twenty years, and individuals from the business world, who are making a complete career change. Many students in the program could be labeled as nontraditional. Some have chosen graduate school, because they are seeking New Jersey Teacher Certification. Most, however, are responding to the problems of isolation and stagnation that tend to be pervasive in the early childhood field, and are seeking alternatives to the inappropriate practices they are frequently expected to implement.All students in the master's program face significant challenges. Most have full time jobs, and many have family responsibilities. Time and energy are limited, and sometimes families are not supportive. In addition, the decision to begin graduate work represents a change in status, which can increase the stress students experience. Without mentoring many students struggle alone. They also remain in danger of not completing the program or not making significant changes in their personal and professional lives (Cox, 1997). Mentoring has the potential to provide the type of support necessary for transformative processes that lead to true change in thought and behavior (Mezirow, 1991).

Informal Peer Mentoring

During her eight years as the graduate coordinator for the Department of Early Childhood and Family Studies, Dr. Ashelman has functioned as the primary mentor. She has also observed and encouraged the development of spontaneous mentoring relationships among students. Many students form loose partnerships based on their need to complete papers or curriculum assignments. This process is referred to as "chumming" (Mullen, 1997, 164). As these groups progress through classes together, informal networking occurs, with students making referrals for jobs and sharing resources and strategies.

Some of the most resourceful students establish dyads in which both participants support each other's development and growth. They complete most of their assignments as a team, and some engage in shared research for their Advanced Seminar project. While open to other friendships, these peer dyads become almost self-sufficient, and each member gives and receives strong support. The positive dynamics of these dyads depend on the pairs' complementary characteristics, similar style of working, and shared interests (Martin, 1998). These informal relationships constitute a strong base for an ongoing peer mentoring program.

In recognition of the importance of peer interaction, the graduate coordinator has encouraged other mentoring relationships among students. One of her most significant efforts has been to arrange study groups for students preparing to take the comprehensive examination. Because of the high anxiety associated with this major test, which determines whether students can complete in the program, the graduate coordinator had a captive audience when she met with the first group. Initially, as the leader of this group, she considered herself to be the sole mentor. Over time, with the intent of diminishing her role as an authority figure and encouraging self reliance, she facilitated the formation of informal student-run study groups.

As students began to work together, they mentored each other in a variety of ways. Members of each group had knowledge and experience to share and varied levels of confidence. Within groups, members took turns playing the role of mentor and protégé, as was appropriate. For the groups that functioned effectively, the graduate coordinator's involvement steadily decreased. In the seven years since these study groups became an integral part of the master's program, problems with successful completion of the comprehensive examination are rare, and the stories of student empowerment and long lasting relationships abound. One account is provided by a former graduate student, Elizabeth Carlson, who graduated in 1994.

> When it was time to prepare for the comprehensive examination, I joined a study group of six people I met in classes. Dr. Ashelman provided general direction for studying, but, for the most part, she made it clear that we were responsible for helping each other. Our group met at each other's homes throughout the summer. We researched theory and theorists and their applications. We discussed possible questions and wrote practice essays. Many points of view were exchanged that helped all of us grow. Overall, it was an incredibly intense and stressful time, which was also invigorating and exciting. We had fun as well. The last night we met was spent at the beach house of one of the group members. Best of all, most of us did exceptionally well on the exam. We also have remained friends and have maintained ongoing professional relationships.

An additional group mentoring opportunity of significance came at the beginning of a research class taught several years ago. The class had been assigned an undesirable room in an isolated part of the campus. Maryanne, a student in the class, extended an invitation to meet at her home the following week. The first session at Maryanne's was such a positive experience, the class did not return to the campus that semester. Outside the university environment, the group dynamics changed. On campus, traditional roles were assumed. In an informal setting, the distance between professor and student was diminished, and opportunities emerged for all group members to participate equally. In this more relaxed setting, research, an unfamiliar topic to this group of students, became less forbidding. When this group of students moved on to their two semester Advanced Seminar research project, they returned to Maryanne's for meetings.

Although the graduate coordinator was the primary mentor to this Advanced Seminar group, the students had numerous opportunities to mentor each other. Throughout the year they took their responsibilities seriously. They critiqued each other's work and provided nurturance when a member of the group had problems. One student in the group, who had dropped out of Advanced Seminar twice, finally completed the task within the group's supportive context. Many members of this group have remained friends and get in touch to provide mentoring for each other in their changing personal and professional lives. In addition, the meetings at Maryanne's house were so positive they encouraged the graduate coordinator to propose a formal mentoring program for all students in the Department Early Childhood and Family Studies.

Formal Mentoring in the Early Childhood and Family Studies Department

At the time the graduate coordinator became interested in developing a formal mentoring program for graduate students, another faculty member, Dr. Arlene Martin, joined the Early Childhood and Family Studies Department as Director of the DART Center, described in Chapter One. During this period, she was engaged in doctoral work at Columbia University, and the topic of her dissertation was mentoring. With her guidance, the graduate coordinator continued to search for ways to facilitate mentoring processes among graduate students. Dr. Martin, a graduate of the department's master's program, suggested enlisting the support of alumni as mentors. This idea appeared to have merit, and it became the central focus for a formal program, designed to extend opportunities for all students to be mentored.

The initial plan for the formal mentoring program was based on previous research with mentor/protégé dyads. It was hoped that each graduate student would be paired with a mentor, selected from a pool of alumni volunteers. With this purpose in mind, alumni mentors were selected, who in turn, participated in defining roles and designing the program. Activities commenced with several group meetings, which were held in the fall, 1997 semester. The purpose of these meetings was to introduce mentors to beginning graduate students in their initial course, Foundations of Early Childhood and Family Studies. While students and mentors clearly benefited from these meetings, no dyads emerged spontaneously. More extensive interactions were arranged with a new group of Foundations students in the spring, 1998 semester. Some students from this group chose mentors and formed dyads.

Feeling the need to provide more opportunities for alumni mentors and students to interact and form bonds, the graduate coordinator decided to include mentoring in her Curriculum Development class during the summer, 1998. An alumni mentor opened her home for selected class meetings. A combination of class assignments that required collaboration between mentors and students were planned. One activity, which involved creating a web for a project, provoked significant interchange and helped validate the practice of integrating mentoring into a specific course. Based on this finding, mentoring was interwoven throughout the Foundations course as a part of the requirements in the fall, 1998. Mentors were asked to work with students on specific assignments, such as field observations, development of a portfolio, and a documentation project.

Documentation as a Means for Introducing Mentoring

The documentation project for the Foundations class required each student or small groups of students to observe in one of the alumni mentor's early childhood job settings. Mentors, who worked in public schools or child care, were identified. Students were asked to develop a documentation project that was in keeping with the following topics listed in *Windows on learning: Documenting young children's work* (Helm, Beneke, and Steinheimer, 1998).

1. Study children's learning in the areas of physical, emotional, social, and/or cognitive development,

2. Examine learning processes involved in the use of integrated approaches such as projects,

3. Record and analyze a child/children's special interests and developmental progress,

4. Demonstrate advantages of concrete, real, and relevant activities and materials to the lives of young children,

5. Assess and evaluate what children know and can or cannot do, showing how instruction is shaped by this information, and

6. Implement innovative practices in a classroom and show how interaction changes and what is learned (24).

Through this documentation project, each student had to interact with at least one alumni mentor during the semester. Therefore, each mentor had the opportunity to model appropriate practices and share expertise with one or more students. This initial contact also served as a point of reference for future meetings.

Portfolios and Mentoring

In addition to documentation, alumni mentors have also become active in assisting students in the process of portfolio development. Portfolios fit well with mentoring, because they provide a complex, multidimensional, and dynamic framework for assessment. Development of metacognitive strategies, student empowerment, and responsive program practice are also supported through this type of assessment (Paulson & Paulson, 1990; Rogers & Danielson, 1996).

Maintaining portfolios serves three primary departmental goals (Ashelman, 1996). First, assessment for graduate students is congruent with the department's position on appropriate practice for young children. Second, instruction and assessment are based on the principles of constructivism, which validate the importance of each student's role in self and shared reflection, goal setting, and personal responsibility for professional growth (DeVries & Kohlberg, 1990; Duff, Brown, & Scoy, 1995). Third, this type of assessment involves faculty and mentors in a collegial process of reflection and critical analysis of program outcomes.

An adaptation of The Cognitive Model for Assessing Portfolios (Paulson & Paulson, 1990) has provided a comprehensive conceptual framework for constructing and evaluating portfolios for graduate students in the Department of Early Childhood and Family Studies (Ashelman & Lenhoff, 1993). This model incorporates three dimensions; Activities, Historical and Stakeholder. The Stakeholder Dimension involves the relationship of mutual investment shared between each student, faculty advisor, and mentor. Student choice supports the concept of active involvement in assessment, as an essential and vital part of the construction of knowledge (Wadlington, 1995). In addition, as the student, faculty advisor, and mentor work together to select and analyze information, each invests time and energy that deepens the commitment of all parties to continued professional growth (Jones, 1993).

The Historical Dimension divides the portfolio process into three phases, which include a baseline record of performance, documentation of changes over time, and summative information that can be used to verify learning outcomes. The three phases of the Historical Dimension are divided between the time spent in introductory or core courses, specialized courses and electives, and the Advanced Seminar research project, which is the culminating experience for students obtaining a master's degree. Involvement of mentors is planned for all three stages. In the first, a documentation project is completed under the supervision of a faculty mentor and an alumni mentor. Alumni and faculty mentors may be involved as integral parts of the support system for the Advanced Seminar project.

The Activities Dimension defines what is to be collected in the portfolio, as well as what is minimally acceptable. Writing, professional development, and teaching practice are the three categories of the Activities Dimension. Multiple samples are collected for each category to strengthen the validity of judgments about performance. Writing, the first category of the Activities Dimension, is a crucial area of development for graduate students. Through the portfolio process, students are encouraged to engage in critiques of their writing through individual and group activities. Process writing, which includes brainstorming, drafting, and editing, is emphasized (Hoskinsson & Thompkins, 1994). Alumni and peer mentoring serves as a support system for students who need assistance in writing.

The second area of the Activities Dimension is professional development. This aspect of the Activities Dimension offers a systematic approach by which students are encouraged to reflect on their own behavior and examine how it corresponds to the standards of the profession (NAEYC, 1991; Duff, Brown, & Scoy, 1995). Leadership and commitment to developmentally appropriate practice have been identified as desired outcomes of the graduate program. Through participation in professional development activities, students' growth in these areas can be documented. Alumni mentors are particularly helpful in providing models of appropriate teaching practices and in supporting emergent leadership and advocacy efforts.The third category of the Activities Dimension is teaching practice which includes simulated and field practice. In specific courses and informal mentoring groups, graduate students simulate classroom practice through working with scenarios, problems and dilemmas, which encourage them to interact collaboratively to evaluate experiences and to debate both personal and professional issues. Field practice focuses on classroom behavior and change at the school level. Shared video analysis of the student as a practitioner, peer observation, and a documented statement about performance from the student's supervisor provide data about growth and development. Documentation projects, completed with the assistance of an alumni mentor, yield some of the most important information about students' field practice.

Collecting and maintaining portfolio samples and artifacts is a cooperative process between the student, faculty advisor, and mentor. Students are responsible for maintaining their portfolio and for giving it a format that is personal and unique to them. In an effort to stimulate creativity and to encourage each student to document his/her own unique journey of personal and professional development, book arts workshops have been offered to all Foundations students. In these workshops, a book artist, with a strong early childhood philosophy, guides students in exploration of varied book forms and formats. She also shows students how to incorporate themes from children's books, as a means for presenting their portfolios in an aesthetically pleasing and distinctive manner. Interest has been so great, a book arts course has been developed and is offered each year with alumni mentors and students enrolled. The book artist has also become a beloved mentor to a growing number of students. In addition, many students are incorporating book arts and portfolios into their classrooms (Ashelman, 1996). This confirms the validity of modeling practices that are congruent with what is appropriate for children, as a means for fostering professional development and change.

Development of a Graduate Mentoring Course

A graduate course entitled, Mentoring in Early Childhood Settings, is an additional component of the department's formal mentoring program. This course was piloted during the fall, 1998 semester, and has been incorporated into the

Administration in Early Childhood Settings Option as a requirement. The purpose of the course is three-fold: 1.) to encourage the formal mentoring of graduate students, 2.) to train graduate students to become mentors in their own work settings as teachers, supervisors, or directors, and 3.) to develop the skills of individuals who serve as alumni mentors. Course content, which is taken partially from the DART Mentor Teacher Curriculum described in Chapter One, is based on adult development, developmental supervision and transformational learning. Conducted in seminar format, the course begins with a consideration of mentoring principles and practices and definitions of mentoring roles and functions. Two seminars follow which address the literature on mentoring and adult development and emphasize the work of Katz (1972), Knowles (1988), Ojo (1980), and Mezirow (1991). Subsequent seminars address stages of mentor development, dimensions of mentoring, and the process of developmental supervision. The literature on supervision includes the writings of Knowles (1980), Caruso and Fawcett (1986) and Glickman (1990). This course offers practical information and strategies for integrating mentoring into students' work settings. Through discussion, role play and a guided mentoring assignment, students learn the roles of mentor and protégé. The course offers opportunities for students to develop mentoring skills, to grow professionally as mentors, and to be mentored by alumni of the program.

Conclusion

The mentoring program in the Department of Early Childhood and Family Studies is a work in progress. It will take additional time and effort to develop a model that serves the needs of all students. At this point, informal and formal mentoring is available to interested students, and the mentoring program has become a strong commitment for some of the department's faculty. The primary goal of the mentoring program is to support growth and change which leads to transformation at the personal and professional level. The next chapter provides five stories of transformation, taken from research on the dynamics of mentor/protégé dyads.

Activity 6

Beginning a Portfolio

Before beginning a professional portfolio as described in this chapter, you might find it useful to construct a general portfolio first, in order to become acquainted to the process. Self assessment is a key to beginning any portfolio project. Teachers, mentors, protégés, and directors should each be able to set the criteria for what is included in a general portfolio, much of which occurs when the author, after thoughtful consultation with peers, decides what to include and exclude from the portfolio.

Things that might be included:

Anything produced by children

Lesson plans

Songs

Poems

Stories, found or written

Articles

Music

Personal thoughts

Artwork

Activities

Field Trip momentos

Photographs

Journal entries

Reflections

Voices from the Field

Profiles of Mentor/Protégé Dyads

Chapter 6

This chapter explores stories of transformation from mentors and protégés in early childhood settings. What is it about mentoring relationships that makes them enduring and transformative? The literature on mentoring has shown that it is difficult to pinpoint the nature of the relationship because it is a different phenomenon. Some researchers have called mentoring "murky business," and hard to define. Thus, there are many definitions for mentoring but no universal one. When considering mentoring, the transformative relationship is most important because of its intimate and in-depth nature (Daloz, 1986; Mezirow, 1991; Cranton, 1994; Martin, 1998).

Natalie Gehrke (1988) states that in order to study mentoring, one needs to conduct what she defines as "affectionate research." In her view, it is not possible to look at mentoring relationships through an experimental lens. She believes that such research must be conducted qualitatively through a lens of the heart. Her perspective reminds one of the story, *The Little Prince,* in which the fox tells the little prince his secret:

> And here is my secret, a very simple secret:
> It is only with the heart that one can see rightly;
> what is essential is invisible to the eye.
>
> — (Saint-Exupery, 1943, 79)

This illustrates Gehrke's concept of "affectionate research" that one must bring one's heart to the study of mentoring or risk missing the essential way of viewing the relationship.

The very nature of the mentoring relationship requires a different way of seeing and a different way of knowing about the phenomenon, precisely because the study of the relationship is bound by intimate, profound experiences and endless sources of self-disclosure. There is a dynamism in this complexity by which the relationship becomes almost therapeutic (Mezirow, 1991,168). This was especially evident for the five mentor/protégé dyads profiled in this chapter. These dyads were interviewed in 1996 as part of a research study on the transformative nature of the mentoring relationship (Martin, 1998). The researcher's role as interviewer and observer was often difficult to maintain because of the compelling discourse and personal interactions that emerged in the interviews.

Each three-way interview was characterized by feelings of genuine caring and respect, by a sense of commitment to each other's process, and by a sense of loyalty to the individual person, akin in some way to a loving relationship. In each session, a feeling that something spiritual had transpired between the dyads was evident in the level of dialogue and disclosure. Some joyful, hopeful experiences emerged in each dyadic interview that validated and affirmed the questions raised in this study. These questions asked what were the perceptions of mentors and protégés about their mentoring experiences and how did their relationships change their personal and professional growth?

In each three-way interview, the sharing of one's experience was like a celebration, and indeed each person thanked the other person for the "gifts" he or she had received in the relationship. One protégé said "I love you, Alex," at the end of her three-way interview. That their experiences were so personal and so moving affirmed the nature and depth of the relationship, which had so touched and changed both mentor and protégé.

In the following section, each three-way interview is interpreted to present a profile and to convey the meaning of the dyad's experience from their perceptions. Each case is preceded by a quality and a saying taken from *Mentoring: The Tao of Giving and Receiving Wisdom* (1995). The quality describes the "feel of the relationship" as perceived from participation in and analysis of audio tapes of the individual interviews, video tapes of the three-way interviews, and field notes. These profiles convey the meaning perspective of the dyad according to Mezirow (1995, 168).

Attentiveness - Grace and Nancy

Attentive listening to others is important regardless of their
stations and positions. Wise people consider the deep meaning
and true value of all suggestions. Learning and teaching are
exchanged joyfully through deep listening and mutual appreciation.

— (*Mentoring: The Tao of Giving and Receiving Wisdom,* 1995, 64)

"Attentiveness" describes the most significant quality of this pair because the mentor, Grace, had a certain quietness and calmness amid her warmth, which emerged as a key ingredient in the effectiveness of the relationship. Her very style was a challenge to Nancy, the protégé, because it contradicted the protégé's own chatty, ebullient personality. Nancy's enthusiasm and different personality from her mentor became evident when she was unable to stop adding just one more thought despite the knowledge that her interview was no longer being recorded. The pair seemed an unlikely match except for the mutual respect and regard they expressed for each other in their three-way interview.

Grace had many years of experience in the field, and though her age and experience set the two participants apart, it also brought them together. It appeared that this mentor's expertise, skills and resources met the needs of this protégé. This was a protégé who expressed her need for her mentor's knowledge. Six months earlier, her only formative experience with children had been as a babysitter. In her mentor's interview, Grace stated repeatedly that Nancy had enormous inner resources, though she lacked skills and confidence in herself. Her insight into the nature of the young child, her limitless creativity and her boundless enthusiasm served her well and endeared her to her mentor.

It was their different personalities that actually made Grace and Nancy a good match, because they balanced each other very well. Each recognized the other's strengths and shortcomings while appreciating the other's gifts. Grace clearly admired Nancy's creative talents, energy and enthusiasm. She stated, "She challenges my creative edge. I learn from her." Nancy clearly appreciated her mentor's patience and "attentiveness" to her needs and the fact that she provided her with a structure in which to organize herself, calling on her to stay on task. From this she learned the importance of self-regulation, a skill most necessary for her to understand what infants and toddlers need to learn in their earliest developmental stages. Nancy stated, "Grace's respect for my process enabled me to learn how to be a support for others."

There was no ego involvement observed in this relationship. There was simply a fondness and a deep appreciation for what both the mentor and protégé brought to the relationship. This theme resonated in each of the five three-way interviews. Because their styles were so very different, both confided that they had done a lot of reflecting on new ideas and ways of doing things. Nancy was able to self-reflect, saying, "My chattiness gets in the way sometimes." She recognized Grace's strength of character and perseverance in keeping her on task, which helped transform Nancy from an unconfident, undisciplined novice to a self-confident, organized and respected teacher.

Non-Judgment - Alex and Danice

Enlightened people do not judge.
Those who judge are not enlightened.
The way of Tao does not distinguish
And works without division and conflict.

— (*Mentoring: The Tao of Giving and Receiving Wisdom*, 1995, 48)

The next dyad, Alex and Danice is characterized by a quality of non-judgment, and of acceptance which was apparent in the three-way interview. The mentor, Alex, provided an environment of safety and nurturance, for children as well as for his protégé. As with the first dyad, this pair seemed an unlikely match: a Caucasian male mentor and an African-American female protégé, whose previous long-term career had been in the insurance industry. A common factor was that they were both of the same age. Both quickly recognized that neither one was pretentious. They both had a singular goal and similar expectations. An endearing feature of Danice's personality was her willingness to participate and be a part of the process immediately. Alex admired her dedication and her ability to jump right in. Danice was eager to be in this relationship, for she sensed at once that she could learn a great deal from him: "I trusted his level of expertise. I saw how he interacted with the children. This is somebody I could learn from."

Alex saw a special quality in Danice, something that told him that she was going to be a terrific teacher. He protected her emotionally and provided her with a safe place to try new strategies, yet he challenged her and pushed her edges. He respected her willingness, even her need to ask a lot of questions, to get to the underlying reasons for understanding his teaching practice. In this interview, Alex shared that mentoring gave him a voice: "It made me realize that I have knowledge and I want to share it with others." He was validated, and his experience, skills and expertise were affirmed.

In her individual interview, Danice was nervous and fairly quiet. As soon as she entered into the three-way interview with Alex present, her demeanor changed from reticent to engaged and reflective. She was calmer and instantly comfortable when her mentor entered into the dialogue. Clearly, Alex validated her mentoring experience. There was evidently real care and concern for each other; a high regard and comfort level were expressed. The interview ended sweetly, with Danice concluding, "I love you, Alex."

This interview was a clear illustration of Gehrke's statement that research on mentoring is "affectionate research." The friendship, closeness, respect, and the non-judgmental feel of the dyad was evident. Further, they had changed the way the other saw themselves in the context of their mentoring relations. They were more than teacher and student, more than friends: they transcended those roles, learned from each other and were changed. That was the meaning of transformation for each of them: that they were different from who they were when they began the process.

Integrity - Maria and Jody

Hold to your ethics and principles.
Stand strongly for what you hold true.
Believe in your true self without compromises.
Trust in the power within yourself and use it.
Act in concert with your dreams and visions.
Cleanse your heart and soul as nature renews itself.
Be honest with yourself and you will be aligned with what
is right, in harmony with the natural laws of the universe.

— (*Mentoring: The Tao of Giving and Receiving Wisdom*, 1995, 40)

This pair was composed of seasoned professionals, so each brought gifts of maturity and expertise to the relationship. And yet there was a reciprocity, a genuine "I-Thou" aspect to the relationship. The protégé, Jody, was completing her degree in early childhood education and had many years of paraprofessional experience, working with young children in Head Start. She acknowledged that she "had to make the experience." She knew that she would get from Maria, her mentor, only as much as she herself gave to the relationship. Both agreed that mentoring offered them a revitalization in their careers and a renewal in their professions. It energized both mentor and protégé. "It's made me want to do so much more. I like helping. I see it as helping the field," said Maria.

Jody likened her experience to an apprenticeship. When questioned about her decision to be mentored rather than participate in a traditional student-teaching experience, she replied, "Why would you want to do it any other way? There's a real value in mentoring." She expressed her belief that mentoring was definitely a valuable experience. She reported that in her college seminar, which contained a mixed group of protégés and student-teachers, the student-teachers often complained of boredom in their roles and were jealous of the mentor/protégé relationships, because they appeared so much deeper than their own student-teaching experiences.

Like her protégé, Maria, her mentor said that she had changed her practice: "I became a better teacher through mentoring because it makes me reflect back on my own teaching practice." When asked what she had gained, she replied, "I have no fear. I have something to share." This theme recurred in other mentor interviews. This dyad presented a clearly comfortable, collegial relationship, one with obvious caring and enjoyment of each other. The willingness and acceptance of both partners to grow together were factors which caused them to expand, reflect and change in each other's reflection, which transformed them both professionally and personally.

The role of advocacy and leadership emerged as a theme within this relationship. Since both partners had been in the field for many years, there was a strong awareness that through mentoring they were now assuming roles of advocacy and leadership in the field of early childhood education. Mezirow (1991) qualifies this as a transformation because there is a change in a meaning perspective that is, in this case, a changed perspective of "self."

Trustfulness - Dawn and Lorraine

Life's unfolding of events is as apparent as the coming and going of the seasons, the alternations of the sun and moon and the stars. All things are exactly as they should be.

— (*Mentoring: The Tao of Giving and Receiving Wisdom*, 1995, 52)

All things as they should be, a sense of well being, a sense of trust: these notions typify the feel of Dawn and Lorraine's relationship. There was a comfortable ease during this interview, as if the two had been together for many years, though their formal mentoring relations had ended six months earlier. Now, as co-workers and friends, they laughed, joked, giggled and sought each other's opinions with mutual regard. More seriously, they expressed their deep appreciation for the relationship, which had changed both of them personally and professionally. As partners, they comfortably shared their fondness for each other and their memories of the beginnings of their relationship.

The mentor, Dawn, an experienced professional in the field, was at the point of making a life change that included the possibility of leaving the field of early childhood education. It was at that point that she became aware of mentoring as a potential next level for her professional life. She disclosed that her mentor training offered her a much-needed renewal. In their quest to develop a trusting relationship, this dyad said they found that a sense of humor helped them achieve that end and truly distinguished their relationship from the other dyads. It set the tone for their relationship and created a space in which they could discuss, debate and move each other to learn new ways. Dawn described her protégé, Lorraine, as having maturity and an ease with herself. She said, "I enjoyed the way Lorraine was with children. She handled feedback well, and took initiative."

In the three-way interview, there was a warmth and a genuine affection for each other. Dawn was a seasoned professional whose decision to remain in the field hinged on her mentor training, as described earlier. She said this training renewed and revitalized her and gave her a new purpose and a new calling to remain connected to the field of early childhood education. It gave her permission to bring herself more fully to this relationship, to be more engaging and full of trust than she had been in other relationships.

Lorraine, the protégé, was significantly younger, a quick learner and an easy communicator. She was very open and reflective in the three-way interview. She disclosed a great deal regarding the transformative effects of mentoring on her life. She felt that her mentor "gave me permission to be myself." More importantly, "Dawn valued her ideas. "Their relationship typified mentoring in the classical sense (Busby, 1989). In her mentoring role, Dawn experienced a validation of her own knowledge, skills and expertise: "I feel good about what I do. I feel valued. It's given me merit." The level of intimacy in this exchange caused her own practice to improve as she became more reflective of her teaching style. It moved her to become more sensitive to the other person's needs in the relationship and, in turn, to become more sensitive to the children under her care and tutelage. As a result of mentoring, she became more compassionate and gentler in her teaching style.

The level of trust and confidence that Dawn instilled changed Lorraine most profoundly. Not only did she say that her practice improved, but that she was able to use her new skills in communication, feedback and reflection in her personal life with her family and in her work in the community. From her perspective, there was initially a mild discomfort in the relationship, because she did not know how she fit into the existing teaching situation in her mentor's program. She had to find her own way, relax, trust and be at ease with the way things were in order to begin to have confidence in herself. This was her path, and this indeed was what she learned from the experience. Mentoring transformed her by enabling her to try new ways in teaching, to grow in her ability to risk in a safe environment, and to know that if it didn't work, she was still OK. This "gift of wisdom" (Gehrke, 1988) imparted from Dawn to Lorraine in the mentoring process provided her with the knowledge of "trustfulness."

Kindness-Hope and Sherry

Loving kindness toward others will create a spirit of unparalleled reciprocity. Followers will become leaders, willing followers jointly overcoming hardship and honoring sacrifice toward mutual goals. With loving kindness, you will win hearts. Through compassion, you will gain loyalty and cooperation.

— (*Mentoring: The Tao of Giving and Receiving Wisdom*, 1995, 44)

Kindness describes this mentor/protégé dyad clearly. There was a high level of comfort in their relationship, as if they were one in spirit, one voice. The mentor, Hope, a warm, open, experienced professional, helped her protégé, Sherry, to feel at ease, enabling her to relax and enjoy the interview process. Hope's maturity, insight and reflective, quiet nature fit well in this mentoring relationship. Sherry, also a mature woman, was known by the mentor prior to their working together. Hope saw her protégé as a strong leader and a voice within their community. She admired this leadership quality, and when she heard that she was in early childhood training as well, she sought Sherry out. An immediate personal connection bonded them in their roles.

This close connection provided an early strength to their relationship. Their communication was very open and well developed. Hope did not push or force the process, but let it happen in its own time. Her style of mentoring utilized open-ended inquiry that helped move the process and allowed the relationship to unfold and develop at its own pace and comfort level. Sherry recalled this questioning practice was a part of how her mentor would guide her into problem-solving and reflective practice.

A major strength of their relationship was the kindness that transpired between them. In that one quality, they were very much alike. Speaking of her practice, Sherry disclosed that the things she learned through mentoring she was able to internalize and bring into her personal life as well. "I'm more of a role model for my own children. They see me as changing some of my speaking patterns, encouraging them. I practiced these skills on my own children."

Both Hope and Sherry talked about the power of mentoring in transforming them personally and professionally, for each of them changed their career goals as a result of the relationship. They are more invested in the field of early childhood education. The awareness that mentoring brought them filtered not only throughout their practice but through all their other relationships. Both of them looked to mentoring to expand their career goals, and they sought to grow as advocates and leaders in the field.

Reflections on Transformation

Mentor/protégé perceptions confirm the process of transformation described in these dyads' relationships. The process of transformation, defined as a natural life event (Nerburn, 1996) in which all things change over time, applies to the growth experienced by the mentors and protégés profiled here. Nerburn asserts the concept of "giving," is a prominent feature of mentoring relationships and states that "giving is a miracle that can transform the heaviest of hearts. The world expands, a moment of goodness is created, and something new comes into being where before there is nothing" (45). Giving is a significant aspect of mentoring, promoting the transformational process in the relationship. Giving and receiving, a part of the process identified as reciprocity, were found within the 16 dimensions of mentoring identified in this research and are listed later in this chapter. These dimensions, as reported by the 10 study participants, confirm that the process of transformation has occurred. They described empowerment, risk and vision, which created, changed and transformed the ordinary events of their professional lives and, similarly, their personal lives. To view daily events through new eyes, to risk new ways of doing, being and communicating-these are the transformations they said affected them through mentoring. The profoundness of the experience was not in its magnitude or even in a quantity of change that could be measured but in the simple practices they learned from each other. These simple truths-of being and becoming in a relationship-were the change agents that transformed both mentor and protégé.

Mentoring transforms individuals through the processes of empowerment, risk and vision, three of the dimensions found in this study of mentor/protégé perceptions. It transforms both mentor and protégé by providing them with opportunities and incentives to challenge them to continually improve their practice and their "professional self." By seeing other ways, they can develop a new vision that moves them beyond their comfort level, to risk-taking and in the process empowers them to become better teachers, professionals, and people. For the mentor, mentoring is transformational in that it renews and revitalizes, or reenergizes the seasoned practitioner, providing a new vision as well. Further, it adds new skills, status and financial reward. Mentoring creates opportunities for personal empowerment and professional growth as both practitioners become more reflective (Mezirow, 169).

For protégés in the relationship, mentoring offers a voice, a place to tell their stories and to be validated in their experiences. The importance of having a "voice" was expressed in each interview and represented a difference between the mentor/protégé relationship and the experience of the student/teacher relationship. Since each protégé shared classes with people who were not being mentored but were in traditional student-teaching roles, the protégés heard and felt these differences when they discussed their relationships during class seminars. Often, the student teachers were envious of the mentor relationships with their protégés. Some wished they had been placed in a mentoring relationship instead of a student-teaching placement. Others felt they had been cheated in their relationships, because they weren't receiving the benefits of mentoring.

Protégés expressed the differences they perceived between mentoring and student-teaching in terms of the regularity of their meetings and that there was a mutual, reciprocal relationship in which each was learning from the other. Most importantly with mentors, protégés had a voice in getting what they needed from the relationship. They viewed student-teaching as a nonreciprocal, one-way relationship in which the student's agenda was set by the cooperating teacher, and as a result, the relationship was imbalanced.

In many pre-service teacher preparation programs, faculty struggle with the issue of how best to balance the relationship of the cooperating teacher as a support teacher with that of the cooperating teacher as a practicum supervisor in the field. Canning (1991) describes her experience with student teaching in the following statement:

> Student teachers, trained to please, to defer to professors and
> supervisors for good grades and positive evaluations, said that
> they had a voice but they had learned to withhold it.

— (Canning, 1991, 19)

Through mentoring, on the other hand, protégés were encouraged to find their voice, to use it and to further challenge their mentors with their voice in the process of inquiry and risk. Experiencing a process on their own allowed them to internalize it differently than if they were told to do something they did not understand. Student teaching can be a difficult experience and one in which practice and theory do not necessarily merge as intended in the student-teaching process. Mentor-teacher relations and the processes embodied in mentoring relations, offer the student/teacher relationship a strategy for attaining a more in-depth relationships and a way to integrate theory and practice.

On Metaphor and Meaning

The metaphors of story, journey and, in a figurative sense, transformation (Daloz, 1983, Levinson, 1978, Gilligan, 1977) permeate the literature on mentoring. Through their voices and in their experiences of personal storytelling, mentors and protégés are able to make meaning of the dynamic and profound experiences they have engaged in and to give voice to the changes or transformations they have perceived as a result of their relationships. This is quite different from the usual student-teaching experience, which at its best should be a good mentoring relationship.

The dimensions found in this study-trust, openness, acceptance, encouragement, support, comfort level, knowledge, expertise, communication, feedback, reflection, reciprocity, mutuality, empowerment, risk and vision-represent the most commonly featured dimensions within the mentoring relationship. In the perceptions of the mentors and protégés interviewed in this study, these 16 dimensions have had transformative effects on their personal and professional growth. So compelling were the mentor/protégé voices and stories, that it was consistently true that the dyads continued to remain personally and professionally connected despite the "formal" ending of their mentoring relationships. There was much validation in the strength and quality, and the depth of the relationship from each person interviewed. Mentors and protégés spoke of weaknesses and shortcomings, and included the reality of their situations, their humanity and the influence of their personalities on the relationships.

Patterns that were generated from interviews showed that certain dimensions surfaced at specific phases of development within the relationship. In Phase 1, the relationship-building period, six dimensions emerged: trust, openness, acceptance, comfort level, encouragement and support. These dimensions clearly built the relationship, forging it to the next level, Phase 2, in which the dimensions of knowledge and expertise built an agenda for the work of the relationship to occur.

In Phase 3, the mentor and protégé were learning their style of dialogue, taking its cue from each others' comfort level. This period, building an information exchange, was defined by communication, feedback and reflection. Phase 4 built on the previous levels, but the dimensions of reciprocity and mutuality appeared throughout the paradigm. In fact, all of the dimensions identified prior to Phase 5 appeared quite regularly throughout the periods. However, the dimensions of empowerment, risk and vision appeared only in the final period, in which the relationship roles begin to shift, signifying the possible ending of the mentoring roles and the onset of transformative effects within the relationship.

Oddly enough, none of the protégé participants suggested that they were saddened by the end of the formal relationship. This may indicate a satisfaction in knowing that they had reached a point of departure with their mentor, ending the need for dependence or simply a recognition that in mature relationships, all participant roles change and become something else. Does each story have an ending when the journey is over? It appears that the mentoring phenomenon has a way of repeating itself over and over again. Each one mentors another. Some of the protégés experienced such powerful changes that they were taking training to become mentors as well. Others were advancing their professional degrees, while some were becoming the leaders and advocates they spoke of in their interviews. The identification of advocacy and leadership through mentoring was a recurrent theme throughout these three-way interviews. Examples of mentor/protégé transformations as advocates and leaders are conceptualized in Chapter 7, Reflections on Mentoring and Transformational Learning.

Activity 7

Create Your Own Case Studies

Mentoring dyads should write in their teacher journals a few sentences about the interactions that took place during the week. They should also document new ideas, or experiences that took place as a direct result of the mentoring relationships. Periodically, all of the dyads should meet and compare "case studies". Hearing about the strengths and frustrations of other pairings can help to build pairs and offer strategies for getting through the rough spots. Dyads can construct case studies for inclusion in a center portfolio that will document the mentoring process as a staff development tool to be used by the center in the future.

Activity 8

Check Your Understanding

Match the qualities on the left with the appropriate phrase on the right.

Attentiveness   Grow in ability to risk
                                 in a safe environment

Non Judgement   Open ended inquiry style

Integrity   Recognizing strengths
                                 and weaknesses

Trustfulness   Learned and changed
                                 from each other

Kindness   Advocacy and leadership

Why are these qualities important?

_____

Are these qualities present among the staff in your center?

_____

How can you build these items into your staff development plan.

_____

Activity 9

Applying Case Studies

Select one of the five case studies reviewed in this chapter to try to discern examples of the phases of the mentoring relationships from the given information.

Phase in Mentoring Relationship	Example from Case Study
Phase in mentoring relationship	
Example from case study	
Comfort level	
Encouragement	
Support	
Knowledge	
Expertise	
Building an information exchange	

Reflections on Mentoring and Transformational Learning

Implications for the Field

Chapter 7

T raining, education and supervision of early childhood staff present many challenges to staff development planners and administrators. Child care personnel frequently come to their positions with limited educational backgrounds. However research indicates that education and training are vital to the delivery of high-quality early childhood services (Whitebook et al, 1988). Furthermore, trained staff are essential to ensuring the mental health and well being of young children in non-maternal settings. Early childhood environments constitute especially difficult circumstances for training and supervision, since routine chores, rigorous daily tasks and the continuity of care needed for providing high-quality relationships demand acquisition of complex, interpersonal skills and an understanding of child development principles. Therefore, formal in-service training and ongoing, regular collaborative supervision are necessary to sustain high quality care.

The transformational power of mentoring has given it a strong role for professional development in the field of early care and education. In essence, mentors generate and regenerate the process of learning and dealing critically and creatively with change that leads to transformation, in themselves and in the field (Bellm, Whitebook & Hnatiuk, 1997, 14). The power of the mentoring relationship is also in the special "I-Thouness" that is present (Buber, 1970). The dimensions of reciprocity and mutuality, which serve to develop an "I-Thou" quality in mentoring, may be missing in other relations. When this happens it removes the "give and take" and the reciprocity that is necessary to change both members of the relationship and lead to transformation. This chapter reviews the fundamental principles of mentoring and summarizes the vital role of transformational learning in mentoring.

Mentoring Builds a Foundation for Growth and Change

Since mentoring offers a way to provide on-site individual staff development, it is crucial to ongoing training of new or beginning teachers in early childhood. Mentoring provides a rationale for the integration of theory and "best practice" and a means to offer staff practical approaches to the personal rigors of caring for and educating young children. Within the mentor/protégé relationship lies a mechanism which is similar to the caregiver/child bond, described by Parkay (1988) as a mirror of the dynamic and powerful parent/child relationship. Mentoring as a "relationship for learning" (Fenichel, 1992, 9) suggests that it is a suitable and practical vehicle for training and supervision among all levels of early childhood staff.

Mentoring Promotes Professional Development and Personal Growth

Mentoring offers the field of early childhood education strategies and supports to professionalize and expand its membership. It has the potential to build advocates and leaders. It gives early childhood mentors revitalization and renewal, which are strong incentives to remain in the field. It provides novice early childhood teachers opportunities to gain knowledge and skills, and new ways to approach their profession. It can increase their self-confidence and self-esteem, improve their practice and make them better professionals. Mentoring relationships can transform the personal and professional domains of both mentor and protégé. They also offer strong promise for professionalization and the expansion of leadership and advocacy roles. In addition, mentoring offers hope for the infusion of mentoring models into teacher preparation and in-service training programs.

In all early childhood settings, the mentor/teacher can provide staff with a supportive, helping relationship. As Gehrke (1988) stated, mentoring relationships can provide depth of knowledge (a gift of wisdom), in practice and theory, within a safe environment, offering the staff member ongoing supervision and regular reflection. They can also help staff develop individual goals and create an awareness of the professional "self," thus promoting professional development.

In Chapter Six, mentor/protégé voices affirmed that mentoring fosters a renewal and revitalization for mentors and that mentoring provides protégés with an apprenticeship in which to learn new approaches, practice emergent skills and build effective ways of communicating. In the mentoring relationships described in the previous chapter, both mentor and protégé gave each other permission to be themselves and in that permission, they were able to risk and create a new vision of themselves. The mentors and protégés in these profiles believed that mentoring empowered them to become advocates and leaders in the field of early care and education. These dyads revealed that mentors were preparing themselves in advocacy and leadership roles, while protégés were preparing to become the next generation of mentors.

Mentor/protégé dyads support psychosocial development leading to personal and professional growth. In individual interviews of the mentor and protégé in the profile "attentiveness," both identified mentoring as helping to build their self-confidence. In that same case, the mentor indicated that "positive feedback promotes confidence" while her protégé indicated that "positive feedback encourages growth and empowers her." In the profile, "non-judgement" the mentor talked about how "mentoring encourages the protégé to risk," and the protégé acknowledged that "mentoring empowered me to look within and allows me to take risks." The mentor in the profile "integrity," stated that "mentoring changed and revitalized me." The protégé in this relationship similarly stated that mentoring "revitalized and reenergized me." Similar perceptions were repeated throughout the other interviews.

Mentoring Changes
Both Mentor and Protégé

Through the essential dimensions of a mentoring relationship, which include trust, acceptance, openness, comfort level, encouragement and support, participants move toward transformation. Mentor/protégé relations provide opportunities for growth and change in a variety of ways. With increased one-on-one time, reflection, discussion of developmentally appropriate practices and problem-solving strategies, mentors and protégés change and grow professionally through improved practice and increased advocacy and leadership roles. Mentors and protégés defined benefits of mentoring as "change." They saw growth of communication skills, for provision of instructional practice, as the content of their mentoring experience in terms of professional development. They also saw growth as change in their personal development, e.g., self-disclosure, greater awareness, willingness to share and be open, and ability to reflect back on the other person's needs. The dimensions of communication, feedback and reflection were as significant to them as the new knowledge and skills they had learned.

Laurent Daloz (1986) poses a theory of transformation based on his own work with adult students. His work is framed in developmental theories and is heavily influenced by William Perry. Daloz views transformation as a developmental journey - a metaphor for change through transformation. For Daloz, transformation equals synthesis, and it is indeed the meaning of growth and change in existing meaning structures to include new ones. Using the work of theorists such as Erikson, Loevinger, Piaget, Kohlberg and Perry, Daloz develops his transformational theory through the lens of a developmental perspective and likens it to the Buddhist concept of "enlightenment." He refers to transformation as "the bottom pulled out" which he suggests is a common description of transformation.

Daloz contends that growth is transformative when the individual yields old structures of meaning making and discards them to add new ones (140). Drawing on Perry's (1968) developmental theory of adult learning, Daloz recounts how the individual at the point of transformation must construe new meaning to move from either/or choices, from polarities to dualities, to multiple perspectives. He believes that true transformation is a synthesis of one's beliefs to form a new "self," through revising old truths and ending old schemes. To describe the process which promotes transformative growth, Daloz states that "tensions are the stuff of growth" (141).

Daloz explains his own understanding of transformation as "containing a tension between and subsequent resolution of contraries" (141). He cites the works of Kegan (1968), Friere (1970) and Levinson (1978) to present a coherent theory of change as growth, through transformation. For each of them, the dialects and the polarities of life events present opportunities to "name" the world (Friere, 1970), to move toward a new integration of each polarity (Levinson, 1978), and to create a life-long dialogue with ourselves and between self and others (Kegan, 1968). These are the central issues of our lives. These notions are powerful and lead individuals to the processes inherent in transformation. From an initial look at Mezirow (1991) and his controversial theory of transformation based on changes in meaning perspectives, to Nerburn's (1996) simplistic version of transformation as a common life event, to Daloz's (1986) notion of transformation as a synthesis of making meaning, these conceptualizations join to move the adult learner to transform. These complex concepts form the basis for a transformation theory which embraces relationship learning and holds that mentoring can promote personal and professional transformation. In this next section, vignettes of students and teachers emphasize how transformational learning emerges through the process of mentoring relationships.

From Practitioner to Graduate Student to Workshop Presenter

Chris, a graduate student in the Kean University Department of Early Childhood and Family Studies, worked with both authors. She describes her professional development as a protégé and her subsequent transformation.

My undergraduate performance was less than stellar, to say the least. I lacked direction and a seriousness of purpose. However, my desire to work with young children remained steadfast and upon graduation, I immediately found myself "teaching" in a corporate child care setting. Within the first year, I was promoted three times and landed in a supervisory role. In retrospect, I was truly young and inexperienced. Approximately six months into this new supervisory role, I was provided the opportunity to participate in the DART Mentor Program at Kean University. It was during that experience that I really began to flourish. Under the tutelage of my mentor, I developed into a confident, competent and highly regarded supervisor and early childhood professional.

After almost seven years and a failed attempt at an administrative promotion, I became disillusioned and frustrated with the corporate infrastructure. Concurrently, my professional learning curve was beginning to flatten and I found myself again lacking focus and direction. It was at this time that I decided to leave corporate child care and continue my education. With nervous reservations, I entered the Master's program in Early Childhood education at Kean University. Within a couple of weeks of my studies, I realized that I had made yet another turning point in my professional career. Quite possibly, the best one yet! I am so challenged both academically and professionally by my new mentor, that I have realized potentials in myself that I never even knew existed. To date, it has been an enlightening and learning filled experience and the opportunities for continued growth are infinite.

Chris presents a profile of a competent, enthusiastic and inquisitive student whose life experience enriches her studies in the graduate program.

Both, the early childhood graduate coordinator and other faculty within the early childhood department are impressed by level of understanding and insight into the nature of the child care field. Chris brings a spirit of inquiry and a sense of advocacy to her studies. She appears to be at a more mature level of professional development and growth than others in the field who have far more years of experience. She is drawn to the child care field and has all the markings of a "leader" waiting to blossom. In an opportunity to begin this mentoring process, her mentor recognized Chris' strengths and invited her to co-present at an out of state regional conference. Chris eagerly accepted the invitation. She jumped at the chance to plan the session with her mentor. She showed insight into the planning process and initiated a direction for the session. On the day of the presentation, she appeared calm, organized and confident, and looked forward to the event. Predictably, she made a strong, practically oriented presentation, and was articulate and poised.

This opportunity to share in professional growth presented a moment when both mentor and protégé recognized the power of the transformative learning process. For her part, the mentor learned to step back, to allow the protégé to emerge and to be fully engaged in the event. There was a reciprocity and mutuality evident. In reflecting on the experience, it was important for the mentor to lose her "self" as ego in the process - while the protégé found her "self." Though both voices were heard, this was a risk for both in their exchange of roles. Both had to trust the other to let go, in order to fulfill the transformational process. In the following mentor/protégé profiles transformative experiences through mentoring are also described.

Detailed in Chapter Six are profiles of mentor/protégé dyads, which describe processes in mentoring relationships. In case 1, Nancy describes her feelings about her mentor's expertise. The following description identifies a transformational learning process for Nancy.

> I learned so much from working with Grace that I knew that I
> needed to know. Just watching Grace's ability to stop in the
> moment, figure out, make a decision...okay this situation means

that so and so... And I'd start hearing the little pieces of knowledge and I'd have that piece and then just by watching her I could start figuring out how she's thinking. So I really model that. That's a crucial piece of what I've learned. I also learned how to have faith in myself. I've learned so much from her. I feel really lucky...really empowered as a student and as a teacher to have this opportunity. I'm really glad I went through it with Grace. The benefit that I feel like I'm experiencing now having done it with you (Grace)...is now we're working together.

In Case 5 of the mentor-protégé dyad profiles, Hope reflects on moments of transformational learning that challenge and encourage her.

I encourage them to risk. I say things... (give them) activities to get them to try new ways. I encourage the person to grow and to achieve. I'm challenged to see where they are. Why aren't they growing? Why aren't they identifying what's happening? How can I help them discover on their own? And it's like I want to be accepting of where people are especially when it's mutual and I see someone really wants to grow. You know I want to help them find the tools so they'll have the tools to take with them. So I allow... I give my mentees, the first time I meet them, I ask what they would like to know about me? What would they like to tell me about their life. I guess the openness, the availability, the trust, letting them be at ease... Sometimes when I know I have the relationship built, and I have a student that obviously had a situation that I see her may be failing at, and I saw her insecurity and I saw her sweating... and then I saw her grasp how to handle it. She kind of looked up at me and I try to nod to them to go ahead, it's okay. To see them go back and try the best they can even though they feel they're half there mentally. It can be just a look between us once you establish that basic trust.

The concept of transformation through mentoring, as reported in the dyad profiles affirms that mentoring is a truly reciprocal, mutually transformative experience. This notion, which is founded on a theory of transformation and based on changes in meaning connections, is confirmed in the voices of both mentors and protégés. That transformation is inherent in a true mentoring relationship is what distinguishes Martin's conceptualization of the process from previous research on mentoring.

In Martin's research (1998), mentors and protégés perceived that sixteen dimensions led to the process of transformation for both mentor and protégé in their personal and professional dimensions. Improvement in mentor and protégé practice was reported as both mentor and protégé interacted in dynamic, authentic ways. They expanded their vision, increased their skills, and changed their self-perceptions through reported increases in self-esteem and self-confidence. Shared interactions and reciprocity taught each partner the idea that "we can teach each other." The protégé's expanded vision of "self" and "other" developed an awareness, a transformation that the "student becomes the teacher" as well. Mentoring means developing one's own identity (Daloz, 1983; Levinson, 1972; Stevenson, 1995).

The participant's words in the mentor/protégé dyad profiles indicate that mentoring provides an intellectual and emotional apprenticeship in early childhood education. Self-knowledge is a benefit of the mentoring relationship. Closeness, friendship and feeling special are others. The transformative process includes building a trusting relationship and being open, comfortable and accepting. It requires an exchange of knowledge and expertise, knowledge being "self" disclosure as well as content. Mentoring as transformational learning requires authentic communication and feedback. Mentoring is different from all other professional relationships, because it contains the dimensions of reciprocity and mutuality. It culminates in a challenge or a change in one's meaning connections leading to empowerment, risk taking and a new vision of "self" and "others," which is known as transformation (Mezirow, 1991; Cranton, 1994; Martin, 1998).

Mentoring Provides Benefits to Both Mentors and Protégés

Mentoring provides a collaborative model which empowers both mentor and protégé. It improves mentor/protégé practice and increases self-perception, self-esteem and self-confidence. It offers renewal in the early childhood field, which in turn helps retain seasoned professionals. Providing a rationale for maintaining more powerful, authentic relationships, mentoring offers additional strategies for training new teachers and offers a support for the traditional student teaching model. Mentoring also grows teachers and creates a context for a powerful learning relationship (Fenichel, 1992).

Elements of Collaboration and Reflection That Support Mentoring

As previously indicated, sixteen dimensions occurred within the process of positive mentoring relationships (Martin, 1998). In order to ensure that these processes occur, mentoring models must provide the elements of time, regularity, collaboration and reflection in the following ways.

- Time - provide release time for all participants.

- Regularity - provide regular, ongoing meetings for the mentor and protégé to build their relationship

- Collaboration - provide for collaborative content so that a reciprocal, mutual relationship can develop

- Reflection - provide opportunities to reflect on one's practice

Mentoring programs are ensured greater success when these program elements are developed and provided for in the implementation of the mentoring model.

Building Mentoring Models
in Early Care and Education

In the previous chapters, applications of mentoring, as they applied to early childhood programs, were described. In adapting aspects of the DART Mentor Teacher Model, it is useful to identify "lessons learned" from the original DART pilot as well as for the resulting pilots in other types of settings. These "lessons learned" inform this discussion of what works in developing future mentoring models in early care and education.

Developing a Strong Content Base

As described in earlier chapters and reinforced by the literature on mentoring, a strong content base provides mentors with a sound preparation for working with protégés or novice teachers. The content base that best prepares mentor/teachers reflects principles of mentoring, a foundation in adult and teacher development, developmentally appropriate practices, and an understanding of developmental supervision, with examples of practice in giving and receiving communication and feedback. Effective strategies in delivering this content base include mini-lecture, case study, role play and communication techniques. Some examples of specific exercises to illustrate these points have been provided at the conclusion of previous chapters.

Making an Effective Mentor/Protégé Match

One of the most challenging aspects of the mentoring dynamic is that of matching a mentor and a protégé. Examples of mentor match strategies were discussed in earlier chapters with the literature favoring informal versus formal mentor/protégé matches. Be assured that there is no one right way to accomplish this goal. Though the literature supports informal mentoring above formal mentoring, mentor/protégé matches will be determined by program needs and may even range from an informal to a formal match process within the same agency. Whatever style of match making is chosen be aware of some aspects that may facilitate this process. From the literature on mentoring and from personal experiences (Martin, 1998) in piloting mentoring projects, it may be concluded that the following features may ensure more successful relations:

- A seasoned "master teacher", preferably older than the protégé or novice teacher.

- A "master teacher" who works with the same grade level or similar ages of children.

- Informal opportunities to meet a variety of "mentor/teachers".

- Provide short biographies of available mentors to novice teachers who are seeking "mentor/teachers".

- Provide elements of time, regularity, collaboration and reflection for mentors and protégés to build and grow their relationships.

In thinking through how a mentoring program will be implemented, it is useful to identify strong "master teachers as mentors" and to create a rationale for mentor/protégé matches. Set criteria for identifying both mentors and protégés and identify barriers or weaknesses ahead of time. These program features will promote a successful mentoring model. Mentoring is a "work in progress." Developing a mentoring model must be viewed in this way. In order to grow and change, risks must be taken and evaluation of the model is necessary.

Conclusion

Mentoring, as a strategy in the professional development of early care and education, can be a significant tool for supporting and assisting new and beginning teachers and also can give renewal and rejuvenation to more experienced teachers (Arin-Krupp, 1985; Killian, 1990; Stevens, 1995). Though it is only within the past ten years that training programs with mentoring components have emerged in early childhood education, these programs suggest promising practices for the field and now are being evaluated for positive outcomes.

Understanding the depth of the mentoring relationship and its powerful transformative effects on both the mentor and the protégé, in personal and professional domains, provides educational institutions with the tools to build "teachers," "leaders" and "advocates" while professionalizing the field. Throughout the interviews with mentor and protégé dyads, described in Chapter Six, individuals reported that mentoring provided opportunities to transform their personal and professional "self." Directions for future research should include similar phenomenological studies on the mentoring relationship to further define its impact on the field of early childhood teacher preparation and practice.

The invitation to improve teacher practice, to prepare better teachers and to professionalize staff in the field of early care and education is open. The suggestions and experiences presented provide an effective approach for training staff and offer opportunities to create dynamic, authentic transformative relationships through mentoring practices. Mentoring is a journey of transformational learning, one that will lead to profound and lasting change. It is hoped that this book will inform the emerging mentoring literature in the field of early care and education and offer some practical suggestions for including mentoring into early childhood programs.

Activity 10

Strategies for Implementing Mentoring Practices in a Staff Development Program

Identify one to two staff members who you perceive to be promising peer mentors, meet with them regularly, at times individually and at other times jointly.

Discuss the role of peer mentoring and that you are interested in developing their mentoring skills. Have them identify one other staff person they would like to mentor. By example have them begin meeting with their selected protégés to discuss DAP, curriculum, parenting issues, any issues which staff are concerned about and need extra support with.

Each week that you meet with your staff as a mentor identify ongoing concerns that you collaboratively agree to work on with them during classroom observation time.

Schedule appointments to meet with your protégés, complete classroom observations and provide on-site supervision in the form of feedback. Then hold a post-conference meeting to offer opportunities to reflect and support the staff member as well as to provide resources to assist them.

References

Anderson, E.M. & Shannon, S. L. (1988). Toward a conceptualization of mentoring. *Journal of Teacher Education,* 39 (1): 38-42.

Arin-Krupp, J. (1981). Mentoring: A means by which teachers become staff developers. *Journal of Staff Development.* 8 (1): 12-15.

Ashelman, P. (1996). Portfolio assessment: An early childhood and family studies model. In Eeva Hujala (Ed.) *Childhood Education International Perspectives.* Oulu, Finland: Finland Association for Childhood Education International.

Ashelman, P. & Lenhoff, R. (1993). Portfolios in early childhood education. In Michael Knight and Denise Gallaro (Eds.). *Portfolio Assessment: Applications of Portfolio Analysis.* New York: University Press of America.

Barnett, W.S. & Boocock, S.S. (eds.) (1998). *Early Care and Education for Children In Poverty.* Albany: SUNY Press.

Belenky, M.F., Clinchy, B.M., Goldberger, N.R. & Tarule, J. (1986). *Women's ways of knowing: The development of self, voice and mind.* New York: Basic Books.

Bellm, D., Whitebook, M. & Hnatiuk, P. (1997). *The early childhood mentoring, curriculum trainer's guide.* Washington, D.C.: The National Center for the Early Childhood Workforce.

_____, (1997). *A handbook for mentors.* Washington, D.C.: The National Center for the Early Childhood Workforce.

Bey, T.M. & Holmes, C.T. (1990). (eds.). *Mentoring: Developing successful new teachers.* Reston, VA: Association of Teacher Educators.

Bird, T. (1985). *From teacher to leader: Training and support for mentor teachers, master teachers, and teacher advisors.* Unpublished manuscript. The Far West Regional Laboratory, San Francisco.

Borko, H. (1986). Clinical teacher education: The induction years. In J.V. Hoffman and S.A. Edwards, eds. *Reality and reform in teacher education.* New York: Random House, 45-63.

Buber, M. (1970). *I and thou.* New York: Schribner.

Burden, P.J. (1982). "Developmental supervision: Reducing teacher stress at different career stages." Paper presented at the annual meeting of the Association of Teacher Educators, Phoenix, AZ.

Busby, M. (1989). *Mentoring: A search for meaning.* Unpublished doctoral dissertation. Teachers College, Columbia University, New York.

Canning, C. (1991). What teachers say about reflection. *Journal of Educational Research.* 48 (6): 18-21.

Caruso, J.J. & Fawcett, M.T. (1986). *Supervision in early childhood education: A developmental perspective.* New York: Teachers College Press.

Center for Career Development in Early Care and Education (1993).*Research and background data on career development.* Wheelock College, Boston.

Clark, C.M. & Wilson, A.L. (1994). Context rationality in Mezirow's theory of transformational learning. *Adult Education Quarterly,* 41 (2): 75-91.

Clay, M. (1991). *Becoming literate: The construction of inner control.* Portsmouth, N.H.: Heinemann

Coelen, C. (1979). *Day care centers in the US: A national profile 1976-1977.* Cambridge, MA.: Abt Books.

Cogan, M. (1973). *Clinical supervision.* Boston: Houghton Mifflin.

Cox, M.D. (1997). Walking the tight rope: The role of mentoring in developing educators as professionals. In C. A. Mullen (Ed.), *Breaking the circle of one: Redefining mentorship in the lives and writings of educators,*. New York: Peter Lang Publishing, Inc., 69-84

Cranton, P. (1994). *Transformational learning in adults.* New York: Jossey-Bass Publishers.

Daloz, (1986). *Effective mentoring.* New York: Jossey-Bass, Pub.

_____, (1983). Mentors: Teachers who make a difference. *Change,* 15 (6): 24-27.

Dante. *The divine comedy.* (Trans. J.D. Sinclair, 1961). New York: Oxford University Press.

De Saint-Exupery, A. (1943). *The little prince.* New York: Harcourt Brace Jovanovich.

DeVries, R. & Kohlberg, L. (1990). *Constructivist early education: Overview and comparisons with other programs.* Washington, D.C.: National Association for the Education of Young Children.

Duff, R.E., Brown, Mac. H., & Scoy, I.J. (1995, May). Reflection and self evaluation: Keys to professional development. *Young Children.* 50, 81, 87.

Erikson, E. (1959). *Identity and the life cycle.* New York: International Press.

_____, (1963). *Childhood and society.* New York: Norton.

_____, (1968). *Identity, youth and crisis.* New York: Norton.

Escalonia, S. (1967), Developmental needs of children under two and one half years old. *In on rearing infants and young children in institutions.* The Children's Bureau Research Reports. #6.

Families and Work Institute. (1993). Interim research report on professional early childhood initiatives. New York.

Feiman-Nemser, S. (1992). Mentoring in context: A comparison of two US programs for beginning teachers. International Journal of *Education Research,* 19 (8): 699-717.

Fenichel, E., ed. (1992). *Learning through supervision and mentorship.* Washington,D.C.: Zero to Three/National Center for Clinical Infant Programs.

Ferrar, H. (1994). Final report, DART Center Training of Trainers Project. New York: Collaborative Ventures, Inc.

Final Report: The DHS Ad Hoc Early Childhood Accreditation Work Group,Report to NJ Department of Human Services and the NJ Child Care Advisory Council, April 1998.

Frede, E.C. (1995). The role of program quality in producing early childhood program benefits. *The Future of Children,* 5 (3), 115-132.

Fuller. F. (1969). Concerns of teachers: A developmental conceptualization. *American Educational Research Journal,* 6 (3): 207-226.

Furtwengler, C. (1995). Beginning teacher programs: Analysis of state actions during the reform era. *Education Policy Analysis,* 3: 1-19.

Galvez-Hjornvik, C. (1986). Mentoring among teachers: A review of the literature. *Journal of Teacher Education,* 37 (1): 190-194.

Ganser, T. (1995). What are the concerns and questions of mentors and beginning teachers? *NASSP Bulletin,* 79 (575): 83-91.

Gehrke, N. (1988). Toward a definition of mentoring among teachers. *Journal of Teacher Education,* 39 (1): 39-41.

_____, (1988). On preserving the essence of mentoring as one form of teacher leadership. *Journal of Teacher Education,* 39 (1): 43-45.

Gehrke, N & Kay, R.S. (1984). Socialization of beginning teachers through mentor-protégé relationships. *Journal of Teacher Education,* 35 (3): 12-14.

Gillet, T.& Halkett, K.A. (1988). RCSB mentor program evaluation: The Policy Implications. *Research and Education.* (ERIC Document Reproduction Service No. ED 291 693).

Gilligan, C. (1977). *In a different voice.* Cambridge, MA.: Harvard University Press.

Glatthorn, A. (1987). Cooperative professional: Peer centered options for Professional growth. Collegial learning (Special issue). *Educational Leadership,* 45 (3): 31-35.

Glickman, C.D. (1990). *Supervision of instruction: A developmental approach* (2nd ed.) Boston: Ally and Bacon.

Glickman, C.D. & Bey, T.M. (1990). Supervision. In W.R. Houston, ed. *Handbook of research on teacher education.* New York: MacMillan.

Gould, R. (1978). *Transformation, growth and change in adult life.* New York: Simon and Schuster.

Gray, W.A. & Gray, M.M. (1985) Synthesis of research on mentoring beginning teachers. *Educational Leadership,* 43 (3): 37-43.

Hardcastle, B. (1988). Spiritual connections: protégés reflections on significant mentorships. *Theory into Practice,* 27 (3): 201-208

Harms, T., Clifford, R. & Cryer, D. (1990) *The Infant/Toddler Environment Rating Scale.* New York: Teacher's College Press.

_____. (1980). *The Early Childhood Environment Rating Scale.* Teacher's College Press.

_____, (1989). *Family Day Care Environment Rating Scale.* Teacher's College Press.

Helm, J.H., Beneke, S. & Steinheimer, K. (1998). *Windows in learning: Documenting young children's work.* New York: Teachers College Press.

Henry, M. & Phillips, C.B. (1997). New directions for non-college/university training. In S. L. Kagan & B. Bowman (Eds.). *Leadership in early care and education.* Washington, D.C.: NAEYC.

Hofferth, S.L. (1996). Child care in the United States today. *The Future of Children,* 6 (2), 41-61

Hofferth, S. (1991). *The national child care survey* 1990. Washington, D.C.: The Urban Institute.

Homer. *The odyssey.* (Trans. R. Fitzgerald, 1961) New York: Doubleday.

Hoskinsson, K., & Thompkins, G. (1994). *Language arts: Content and teaching strategies.* New York: Merrill.

Houston, R. W., ed. (1990). *Handbook of research on teacher education.* New York: MacMillan Publishing Co.

Howey, K.R. (1985). Six major functions of staff development: An expanded imperative. *Journal of Teacher Education,* 36 (1): 58-64.

Huang, C. & Lynch, J. (1995). *Mentoring: The tao of giving and receiving wisdom.* San Francisco: HarperCollins.

Huffman, G & Leak, S. (1986). Beginning teachers' perceptions of mentors. *Journal of Teacher Education,* 37 (1): 22-25.

Hughey, J.B. (1997). Creating a circle of many: Mentoring and the preservice teacher. In C.A. Mullen (Ed.), *Breaking the circle of one: Redefining mentorship in the lives and writings of educators,* New York: Peter Lang Publishing, Inc., 101-118.

Huling-Austin, L.S. (1992). Research on learning to teach: Implications for teacher induction and mentoring programs. *Journal of Teacher Education,* 43 (3): 173-180.

Huling-Austin, L., Odell, S., Ishler, P., Kay, R. & Edefelt, R. (1989). *Assisting the beginning teacher.* Reston, VA: Association of Teacher Educators.

Huling-Austin, L. (1986). What can and cannot be reasonably expected of teacher induction programs. *Journal of Teacher Education,* 37 (1): 2-5.

Hunt, D.E. (1966). A conceptual systems change model and its application to education. In O.J. Harvey (Ed.). *Experience, structure and adaptability.* New York: Springer-Berlag, 277-302.

Hyde, L. (1979). *The gift: Imagination and the erotic life of property.* New York: Vintage Books.

Jarmin, H.R. & Mackiel, D.S. (1993). Mentor perceptions of contact with beginning teachers. *The Clearing House,* 67 (1): 45-48.

Johnson, J & McCracken, J. (1994). (eds.). *The early childhood career lattice: Perspectives on professional development.* Washington, D.C.: National Association for the Education of Young Children.

Johnston, J. & Ryan, K. (eds.). (1983). *Research on the beginning teacher: Implications for teacher education.* New York: Longman.

Jones, E. (1986). *Teaching adults.* Washington, D.C.: NAEYC.

_____, (1993). Introduction: Growing teachers. In E. Jones (Ed.) *Growing teachers: Partnerships in staff development.* Washington, DC: National Association for the Education of Young Children.

Joyce, B.R. & Showers, B. (1982). The coaching of teaching. *Educational Leadership,* 40: 4-10.

Kagan, D. (1992). Professional growth among preservice teachers and beginning teachers. *Review of Educational Research,* 62 (2):129-169.

Kagan, S. (1997). *Not by chance: Creating an early care education system for America's children.* Full Report of the Quality 2000 Initiative. New Haven, CT, Yale University Bush Center in Child Development and Social Policy.

Katz, L. (1972). Developmental stages of preschool teachers. *Elementary School Journal,* 73: 50-54.

Kay, R.S. (1990). Mentoring: Definition, principles and applications. In T.M. Bey and C.T. Holmes, eds. *Mentoring developing successful new teachers.* Reston, VA: Association of Teacher Educators.

Kegan, R. (1982). *The evolving self: Problem and process in human development.* Cambridge, MA: Harvard University Press.

Kerr, D.H. (1993). Beyond education: In search of nature. Work in Progress Series, No. 2. Seattle, WA: Institute for Educational Inquiry.

Killian, J. (1990). The benefits of an induction program for experienced teachers. *Journal of Staff Development,* 11 (4): 34-36.

Kohlberg, L. (1981). *The philosophy of moral development.* New York: Harper & Row.

Knowles, M.S. (1980). *Modern practice of adult education from pedagogy to andragogy.* Chicago: Follet Pub. Co.

Kontos, S., Howes, C., Shinn, M. & Galinsky, E. (1994). *Quality in family child care.* New York: Teachers College Press.

Kram, K.E. (1983). Phases of the mentor relationship. *Academy of Management Journal,* 25 (4): 608-625.

Levine, S.L. (1987). Understanding life cycle issues: A resource for school leaders. *Journal of Teacher Education,* 169 (1): 7-19.

Levinson, D. (1978). *The seasons of a man's life.* New York: Knopf.

Levinson, D., Darrow, C., Klein, E., Levinson, M. & McKee, B. (1978). *The season's of a man's life.* New York: Knopf.

Lindamond, J. (1993). Mentoring in early childhood programs. *Journal of Teacher Education,* 14 (2): 21-24.

Mahler, M. (1974). *The psychological birth of the human infant.* New York: Basic Books Inc.

Martin, A. (1998). Transformative dimensions of mentoring: A study of early childhood teachers' perceptions. Doctoral dissertation. New York: Teachers College, Columbia University.

McPartland, C. (1985). The myth of the mentor. *Campus Voice,* 2 (1): 8-11.

Merriam, S.B. (1991). *Case study research in education: A qualitative approach.* San Francisco: Jossey-Bass Publishers.

Merriam, S. (1983). Mentors and protégés: A critical review of the literature. *Adult Education Quarterly,* 33 (3): 161-173.

Merriam, S. & Caffarella, R. (1991). *Learning in adulthood.* San Francisco: Jossey-Bass Publishers.

_____, (1994). Understanding transformation theory. *Adult Education Quarterly,* 44 (4): 222-232.

Mullen, C.A. (1997). Post-sharkdom: An alternative form of mentoring for teacher educators. In C.A. Mullen (Ed.), *Breaking the circle of one: Redefining mentorship in the lives and writings of educators,* New York: Peter Lang Publishing, Inc., 145-174.

National Association for the Education of Young Children. (1991). Position statement on guidelines for appropriate curriculum content and assessment of children ages 3 through 8. *Young Children,* 46, 21, 37.

National Association for the Education of Young Children. (1992). First Critique of Accreditation Folio, Washington, D.C.: NAEYC

National Center for Research on Teacher Education (1988). Teacher education and learning to teach: A research agenda. *Journal of Teacher Education,* 39 (6): 27-32.

Nelson, F. & Restaino-Kelly, A. (1995) Profiles of a fledgling mentor teacher program in *Profiles in Professional Development,* a monograph of the DART Center, Kean University, Union, NJ.

Nerburn, K. (1996). *Simple truths.* Novato, Ca.: New World Library. New Jersey Department of Human Services Ad Hoc Early Childhood Accreditation Work Group (April, 1998).

Noddings, N. (1984). *Caring: A feminist approach to ethics and moral education.* Berkeley: University of California Press.

Odell, S.J. & Ferraro, D.P. (1992). Teacher mentoring and teacher retention. *Journal of Teacher Education,* 43 (3): 200-204.

Odell, S.J. (1990). Support for new teachers. In T.M. Bey and C.T. Holmes, eds. *Mentoring: Developing successful new teachers.* Reston, VA: Association of Teacher Educators.

_____, (1997). Teacher induction: Rationale and issues. In D. Brook (Ed.). *Teacher induction: A new beginning.* Reston, VA: Association of Teacher Educators.

_____, (1986a). A model university-school system collaboration in teacher induction. *Kappa Delta Pi Record.* (4), 120-121.

_____, (1986b). Developing support programs for beginning teachers. In R.A. Edefelt, ed. *Beginning teacher assistance programs.* Reston, VA: Association of Teacher Educators.

Oja, S.N. (1980). Adult development is implicit in staff development. *Journal of Staff Development,* 1 (2): 8-55.

O'Neill, J.H. (1981). *Toward a theory and practice of mentoring in psychology.* In J. H. O'Neill and L.S. Wrightsman. *Mentoring, Psychological, Personal and Career Implications.* Symposium presented at the annual meeting of the American Psychological Association.

Paulson, L. & Paulson, P. (1990). *How do portfolios measure up? A cognitive model for assessing portfolios.* Union, WA: Paper presented at the Annual Meeting of the Northwest Evaluation Association (ERIC Document Reproduction Service, No. ED 334251).

Parkay, F.W. (1988). Reflections of a protégé. *Theory into practice,* 27 (3): 195-200.

Phillips-Jones, L. (1982). *Mentor and protégés.* New York: Arbor House.

Phillips, L. (1977). Mentors and protégés: A study of the career development of women and managers and executives in business and industry. Doctoral dissertation. Los Angeles, CA: University of California.

Piaget, J. (1952). *Origins of intelligence in children.* New York: International Universities Press.

Report: *Indicators of Quality in Early Care and Education.* An issue paper. The Professional Development Committee of the New Jersey Child Care Advisory Council, July 1998.

Restaino-Kelly, A. & Handler, J. (1996). The DART mentor teacher model: Training early childhood supervisors to assist beginning teachers. In Eva Hujala (Ed.) *Childhood Education: International Perspectives*, Oula, Finland: Finland Association for Childhood Education International.

Restaino-Kelly, A. & Rudolph, E. (1997). Building literacy through child development. Iowa: Kendall-Hunt Publishing Company

Ruopp, R., Travers, J., Glantz, F. & Coelen, C. (1979). *Children at the center.* Cambridge, MA.: Abt Associates.

Ryan, K. (1986). The induction of new teachers. Phi Delta Kappa Fastbacks, (237). Bloomington, Ind: Phi Delta Kappa Educational Foundation.

Schein, E.H. (1978). *Socialization and learning to work. Career dynamics: Matching individual and organizational needs.* Reading, MA: Addison-Wesley.

Sheehy, G. (1976). *Passages: Predictable crises of adult life.* New York: E.P. Dutton.

Shulman, J.H. & Colbert, J.A. (1988). (eds.) *Mentor teacher casebook.* Far West Regional Laboratory for Educational Research. San Francisco.

Sprinthall, N. & Thies-Sprinthall, L. (1983). The teacher as an adult learner: A cognitive-developmental view. In G. Griffin, (ed.) *Staff development.* Chicago: University of Chicago Press.

Sprinthall, N. & Thies-Sprinthall, L. (1983). The teacher as an adult learner: A cognitive-developmental view" In G. Griffin, (ed.) *Staff development*. Chicago: University of Chicago Press.

Stansell, J. E. (1997). Mentors and mentoring: Reflections of a circle with/in circles. In C.A. Mullen (Ed.), *Breaking the circle of one: Redefining mentorship in the lives and writings of educators*. New York: Peter Lang Publishing, Inc., 121-144.

Stern, D. (1985). *The first relationship*. New York: Basic Books Inc.

_____, (1987). *The interpersonal world of the infant: A view from psychoanalysis and developmental pschology*. New York: Basic Books, Inc.

Stevens, N. (1995). R and r for mentors: Renewal and reaffirmation for mentors as benefits from the mentoring experience. *Educational Horizons, 73* (3): 130-137.

Theis-Sprinthall, L. (1987). Experienced teachers: Agents for revitalization and renewal as mentors and teacher educator. *Journal of Teacher Education,* 169 (1): 65-79.

_____, (1986). A collaborative approach for mentor training: A working model. *Journal of Teacher Education,* 37 (6): 13-20.

_____, (1981). A cognitive-developmental perspective. In Griffin, G. (ed.) Alternate perspectives for program development and teacher education. Summary of proceedings of an invited symposium for the annual meeting of the American Educational Research Association, Los Angeles, CA.

Veenman, S. (1984). Perceived problems of beginning teachers. *Review of Educational Research,* 54 (2): 143-178.

Ward, B.A. (1986). State and district structures to support initial year of teaching programs. In G.A. Griffin and S. Millies, eds., *The first year of teaching: Background papers and a proposal,* 35-64. University of Illinois and Illinois State Board of Education, Chicago.

Warrington, D. & Linquist, M. (1989). A collaborative mentor-mentee program based in the Bloomington, MN, Public School. *Research and Education.* (ERIC Document Reproduction Service NO. ED 305-328).

Whitebook, M. & Bellm, D. (1996). Mentoring for early childhood teachers and provider: Building and extending tradition. *Young Children.*

Whitebook, M. & Sakai, L. (1995). *The potential of mentoring: An assessment of the California Early Childhood Mentor Teacher Program.* A report by the National Center for the Early Childhood Workforce.

Whitebook, M., Hnatiuk, P. & Bellm, D. (1994). *Mentoring in early care and education: Refining an emerging career path.* Washington, D.C.: National Center for the Early Childhood Workforce.

Whitebook, M., Howes, C. & Phillips, D. (1989). *Who cares? Child care teachers and the quality of care in America.* The National Child Care Staffing Study, Oakland, CA: The Child Care Employee Project.

Williamson, S. (1998). Establishing a mentor program in family childcare. *Profiles in Professional Development.* A monograph of the DART Center, Kean University, Union, NJ.

Zeichner, K. (1983). Alternative paradigms of teacher education. *Journal of Teacher Education,* 34 (3): 3-9.

Zey, M.G. (1984). *The mentor connection.* Homestead, IL: Dow Jones-Irwin.

Wadlington, E. (1995, May). Basing early childhood teacher education on adult education principles. *Young Children.* 50. 76-80.

Zimpher, N.L. & Reiger, S.R. (1988). Mentoring teachers: What are the issues? *Theory into Practice,* 27 (3): 175-181.

Zucker, D.S. (1982). *The mentor/protégé relationship: A phenomenological inquiry.* Unpublished doctoral dissertation. Professional School for Humanistic Studies. San Francisco.

About the Authors

Arlene Martin is Director of the DART Center and Assistant Professor in the Department of Early Childhood and Family Studies, Kean University, Union, New Jersey. She is the co-founder of the Coalition of Infant/Toddler Educators (CITE) a statewide advocacy organization in New Jersey. Her research interests focus on infant/toddler development, training of paraprofessionals in the field of early care and education, and the development of research on mentoring in early childhood. She presents nationally and internationally on mentoring and has previously written *Building Literacy Through Child Development* (1997).

Polly Ashelman is an Associate Professor, and she is also the Graduate Coordinator in the Department of Early Childhood and Family Studies, Kean University, Union, New Jersey. She provides leadership and mentorship to all graduate students in the Master's Program in Early Childhood and Family Studies. Her research interests include documentation, assessment, and early childhood history, and she has published articles related to these topics. She is active in professional associations, and she also presents nationally and internationally.